the complete guide to the

kitten

the complete guide to the
kitten
sarah whitehead

BARNES
&NOBLE
BOOKS
NEW YORK

Complete Guide to the Kitten

This edition published by Barnes & Noble, Inc., by arrangement with Thalamus Publishing.

2000 Barnes & Noble Books

M 10 9 8 7 6 5 4 3 2 1
ISBN 0-7607-2316-8

Commissioning editor: Lucian Randall
Project editor: Warren Lapworth
Jacket design: Thalamus Studios
Interior design: Paul Chubb
Four-color separation: Prima Media Ltd

Printed and bound in India by Thomson Press

Picture Acknowledgments
Picture research by Image Select International Limited
Images Colour Library: 37; RSPCA Photolibrary: (Geoff du Feu) 9, (Cheryl A Ertelt) 90, (Angela Hampton) 2–3, 16, 25, 48, 56, 57, 58, 60, 68, 91, 94, 102, 108, 130, 137, (EA Janes) 7, (Ken McKay) 96, (D Muscroft) 30, (Alan Robinson) 45 bottom, 46, 47 bottom; Spectrum Colour Library: 20, 23, 29 bottom, 43 top, 43 bottom, 44, 80, 92, 99, 100, 117 top, 128, (Anne Cumbers) 38, 42, 47 top, 49, 88, 97, (Mrs JM Lochhead) 109; SuperStock: 143; Warren Photographic 1, 6, 8, 10, 11, 12, 13, 14, 15, 17, 18, 19, 21, 22, 24, 26, 27, 28, 29 top, 31, 32–33, 33 bottom, 34, 35, 36, 39, 40, 41, 45 top, 50, 51, 52, 53, 54, 55, 59, 61, 62, 63, 64, 65, 66, 67, 69 top, 69 bottom, 70, 71, 72, 73, 74, 75, 76, 77, 78, 79, 81, 82, 83, 84, 85, 86, 87, 89, 93, 95 top, 95 bottom, 98, 101, 103, 104, 105, 106–107, 107 top, 110, 111, 112, 113, 114, 115, 116–117, 118, 119, 120, 121, 122, 123, 124, 125, 126, 127 top, 127 bottom, 129, 131, 132 top–133, 132 bottom, 134, 135, 136, 138, 139, 140, 141, 142.

table of **contents**

introduction

From the first day that you bring a kitten into your home, you will be aware that you are sharing your life with a creature that is both wild and domestic. Even at the earliest age, kittens show remarkable prowess in climbing, stalking, chasing, and hunting—yet they usually want to curl up on your lap afterward!

For the past 4,000 years, humans have been adopted by cats! We offer them food, shelter, security, and a unique parental relationship, yet they can walk away at any moment and fend for themselves perfectly well. This remarkable combination of independence and dependency is one of the things that draws so many people to cats in the first place, and what maintains their fascination throughout their pet's life span.

Kittens become cats at a rate that makes their growth almost visible. That cute bundle of fluff may look vulnerable and helpless, but in only a few weeks he or she will have the looks and behavior of a true predator. Cats are built with hunting alone in mind. Their bodies are lithe, powerful, and elastic, their weaponry impressive. Few other animals boast such intricately shaped claws that can be sheathed in order to protect them, or teeth that can kill prey so efficiently.

Cats' senses are fine-tuned to locate prey and detect potential danger, with ears that can rotate a full 180 degrees and olfactory powers that allow them to taste and smell even the faintest odor at the same time.

right *Life is an adventure!*

below *At one week old this kitten is still blind and deaf, but can feel the warmth of a human hand.*

above *Cats have remained largely unchanged through centuries of domestication.*

Cats' abilities as solitary hunters have made them extraordinarily successful. Across the world their adaptability has allowed them to take advantage of human progress and move with people wherever they have ventured. Throughout these travels, the cat's body has barely changed. Only variations in color, coat length, and the occasional difference in tail or head shape have occurred, proving that the original blueprint could hardly be improved.

the cat's history

History tells us that cats have co-existed with man since 1500 BC. Archeological evidence from Ancient Egypt has revealed that cats, little different in appearance to our own today, were mummified to accompany their deceased owners on their trip to the afterlife.

These cats were likely to have been descendants of the African Wild Cat (*Felis sylvestris lybica*) that had undergone a slight genetic shift. This change had reduced the cats' fearfulness of man and allowed them to live in close proximity with us, feeding on prey that was attracted by grain stores and human waste.

Evidence that the African Wild Cat was our domestic cat's ancestor is strong, as even today these wild animals are found among tribes of people in their native land. Interestingly, DNA of these African Wild Cats is indistinguishable from our pet cats, while other species, such as the European Wild Cat, show considerable differences.

With their ancestry in mind, it is easy to see why our domestic cats have retained so much of their original behavior. Even cats that are well-fed, well-housed, and well-loved show the need to go through hunting sequences. This is one of the reasons why so many cats have behavioral problems.

Living in our homes, particularly in urban areas, cats still need to demonstrate natural behaviors. Kittens and cats need to rest peacefully without fear of attack, urinate, and defecate. They also need to stalk, chase, pounce, and climb. Hunting activities would normally be performed 20 to 30 times a day in the wild. In a domestic household this may be severely reduced, or even prevented altogether if the cat is kept permanently indoors and without other forms of play or simulated hunting.

Sadly, while most cats are highly adaptable, humans are not. This means that unacceptable behavior in the home is rarely tolerated, and the causes rarely explored.

understanding your kitten

Understanding why your kitten behaves as he or she does is the single most important factor in the prevention of behavioral problems, both at this early stage and later. This understanding will lead to a further appreciation of the cat as a pet and as an independent character, perfectly capable of forming lasting relationships with its own kind, humans, and other animals.

Attachment in cats is the essential reason why most are kept as pets. Despite their wild side, kittens regard their human owners as surrogate mothers, and this association continues into old age. Even adult cats love to be petted, fed, and spoken to by their owners, and form deep and lasting bonds with their family and home. Some cats are so bonded to their owners that they cannot bear to be parted from them, while others are so attached to their home environment that they travel vast distances to return there, even if they have been offered all the same love and care in a different place!

Cats live in a world that we can only imagine. Their perspective of their environment, and of us, is governed by senses that are far more sensitive than ours. Cats take in much of their information about the world around them via smell, reading the odors that humans and other cats produce as if they were words in a newspaper. Our understanding of how cats interpret this information and how we can utilize it to form closer relationships with our pets is in its infancy, but is already proving useful.

This book is intended to help you have the most positive and enjoyable relationship with your cat. The time that your cat is a kitten is short indeed. Watching him or her stalking a leaf in the wind, playing with a toy, sleeping peacefully by the fire, or cuddled up on your lap will more than reward you for the time, effort, and commitment that it takes to raise a happy, confident kitten in today's hectic world. Enjoy!

below *Kittens become life-long friends.*

9

birth and the first week

Kittens are born blind, deaf, and unable to regulate their body temperature. Despite developing in their mother's womb for approximately 65 days, once born they are still totally dependent on their mother for survival, and cannot even urinate or defecate without her help to stimulate these functions.

However, they do have two powerful abilities—and just one look at the size of a kitten's nose compared to the rest of its face and body at this age gives one of these away! Despite the fact that the kitten's sense of smell is not fully developed until three weeks of age, kittens are able to detect the smell of their mother's saliva in order to locate a teat. Once there, they use a rooting reflex to burrow and will suckle on any object. Even more impressive, they are able to locate a source of heat and can detect the warmth of their mother's body and move relatively long distances toward it in order to sleep or suckle.

below *Still damp from birth, these kittens are cleaned by their mother*

Neonatal kittens move around by crawling. They are unable to stand, and need to use their heads in a strange swaying movement to help guide them and propel them along on their bellies.

Most kittens weigh between 4 and 4.8 ounces at birth. Their weight usually doubles during the first week! This is because feeding and sleeping dominate the kittens' lives. The queen (mother) provides as many meals as the kittens need and spends a great deal of time cleaning them and licking to stimulate the elimination of waste matter.

early instincts and abilities

At this stage, kittens may develop a preference for feeding from a specific teat. He or she may have to wait to feed from their "favorite" and will attempt to push other kittens out of the way to get to it!

Cats are famous for their self-righting reflex, which means that they can twist in the air and land on their feet as they fall. However, this motor skill does not develop until the kitten is much older—usually between four and six weeks of age. However, even directly after birth, kittens can right themselves if they are knocked onto their backs—a skilful and necessary survival strategy.

From birth, kittens are able to purr, and this is probably for useful communication between kitten and mother to let her know when her offspring is successfully feeding. They are also able to emit distress cries, which let the mother know if a kitten is stranded, cold, hungry, or is accidentally trapped underneath her or a sibling.

The neonatal period, as the stage of development between birth and ten days old is called, is a fundamental one. Although the kittens are at a very early stage of development, they are able to smell and feel. This means that input from humans can be a useful strategy if the kittens are to grow up as sociable, outgoing cats. Gently holding each kitten and stroking him or her is enough at this stage, with a quick check to make sure the kitten is healthy. Confident mothers should not be distressed about this, so long as they can see that their kitten is safe.

first week to second week

Over the first two weeks of life kittens continue to grow and develop at an incredible rate. Their eyes begin to open at around ten days old, and although their vision is not yet perfect, they can see their mother, littermates, and the world around them.

The kitten's hearing also begins to develop. The ear canals open at around one week of age, but hearing is not fully operational until the kitten is four weeks old.

Movement is less snake-like and closer to cat movement. Although kittens cannot walk properly until about 17 days, they begin to utilize their front legs to help drag themselves along, particularly to feed or snuggle up with their littermates to sleep.

Feeding is still vitally important, and the rooting reflex becomes more refined. This means that kittens can no longer be fooled into suckling on

above *Kittens huddle together for warmth and security. Littermates often do this later in life.*

fingers and will only attach themselves to their mother's teats.

At this age kittens often show a treading action while suckling. This behavior, called kneading, is thought to help stimulate the mother's milk flow. Interestingly, some cats retain this behavior right through their adult lives, and may demonstrate it when

below *Burmese kittens at two days old.*

cuddled later by their surrogate mothers—us! Indeed, some cats are so convinced that they are in "suckling mode" when held by their owners that they not only knead us, but also salivate in anticipation!

mother's actions

When the kittens are a few days old, the mother may suddenly decide that she wants to move her nest site. This behavior is driven by an instinct to keep the kittens safe by not staying in the same place for too long. In order to move the kittens, the mother usually grasps them firmly by the scruff of the neck and picks them up. Kittens have an innate response to this feeling, and will lie completely still and limp while being carried. Many cats retain this response into adulthood, which can be useful if they need to be handled in an emergency.

Kittens are born without teeth, but these quickly develop. By 14 days of age, their deciduous or milk teeth are beginning to appear, in readiness for the solid food to come. The appearance of teeth may also trigger the weaning process for the mother, as they are extremely sharp and can cause considerable discomfort during suckling.

Continued exposure to the sights, sounds, smell, and touch of people is ideal at this stage of a kitten's development. Further gentle handling, as well as stroking and touching, can ensure that the kittens respond well to human attention later on.

2–4 weeks

The period between ten days and three weeks in kittens is called the transitional phase—and little wonder, as so many changes are now taking place. At this point, kittens can stand and take a few tentative steps. Their milk teeth are coming in, which means that they will make some attempts to chew on solid food by copying their mother.

The kittens' eyes and ears are open and gradually improve with each day, and they can follow moving objects and react to loud sounds. Kittens of three to four weeks of age also begin to gain control over urination and defecation, and start to orientate toward using litter in a box, if it is placed a little way from the nest. Watching and copying their mother using the box is an important part of this learning process.

As soon as the kittens become sufficiently mobile, play between them starts in earnest. To begin with, their games are slow and clumsy, but they soon progress into ambushing each other and pouncing on their mother's tail. Kittens of between three and four weeks start to bite each other in play, and need to learn to moderate the strength of their bite by finding out what hurts and what doesn't!

Weaning starts in earnest at around four weeks of age. This is a very important behavioral and physical stage for the kittens as it marks their growing independence and their ability to cope with frustration (see pages 28–29).

socialization begins

The onset of weaning also seems to coincide with a change in the kittens' play, as they will start to play more with objects and toys than with each other. This represents practice for hunting expeditions in the future—a vital part of becoming an independent hunter.

Despite being fed several good meals a day, the majority of domestic cats retain their hunting instincts, and many queens bring live prey back to the nest to teach their kittens how to develop these skills.

At two weeks' of age kittens enter the socialization phase. This period lasts only until seven weeks and helps to determine how the cat behaves for the rest of his or her life. During this

left *At only 21 days kittens can communicate.*

time, kittens need to be handled by as many different people as possible, discovering that all kinds of humans— large and small, black and white, male and female—are friendly and non-threatening (see pages 24–25).

At this stage, kittens show very little fear—they are programmed to explore and discover the joys of the world. This offers them a window of opportunity to become familiar with many different aspects of domestic life, so it is essential that they are

above *To encourage the start of the weaning process, the queen spends less time with her kittens.*

exposed to these stimuli during this time (see pages 26–27). Kittens that are kept in sterile, under-stimulating environments may show signs of this deprivation in their behavior later on. Sadly, once this period has passed at seven weeks, there may be little that can be done to rebuild the under-socialized kitten's confidence.

4–7 weeks

At around five weeks of age, kittens can run and balance with ease. Climbing is also tackled with great gusto—particularly if the opportunity to scale drapes or furniture prevails. These skills are still being perfected, however, and it is not unusual for a kitten to tumble while practicing.

Five-week-old kittens are pretty independent. They can feed on solid food for themselves, are able to relieve themselves at will, and can groom themselves and their littermates effectively.

Social play starts to take on a slightly more competitive edge, and this is when kittens need to learn how to moderate their play if they are not to be misunderstood later in life. Full-on attacks by one kitten on another are less acceptable, as teeth and claws

do damage, therefore such ambushes are usually moderated in favor of rearing up or darting away. Play with objects such as toys or drapes continues to develop, and stalking and pouncing behaviors—in preparation for hunting—are being perfected.

Kittens of five weeks old and beyond look like miniature cats. They are fully capable of using a range of facial expressions and body postures when communicating with each other and with humans. Their responses to people and to other animals, such as dogs, are more consistent, as they have the opportunity to practice their behaviors with them and regard them as part of their family.

breed and breeder factors

Different litters of kittens are likely to develop at different rates. Breed characteristics may have an influence—as Orientals and Burmese cats are often regarded as precocious. However, far more important, the kitten's rate of physical development is linked to their environment and rearing.

For example, research has shown that kittens that are handled and stroked daily in the first few weeks of life usually show more rapid physical and social development than those which are not, as well as being more responsive to handling by humans later in life. Equally, kittens that are raised in enriched environments, such as the heart of a household, are more likely

to open their eyes and move around sooner than those who are not.

As most kittens remain with their breeder until at least eight weeks of age, full responsibility for socialization and habituation during the critical period lies with them. This is why choosing the right breeder is so important.

At seven weeks old most kittens are independent enough that they are happy to leave their mother and littermates at eight weeks. Pedigree cats cannot usually leave their mother until 12 weeks, so social play continues for longer. However, it is essential that such kittens also receive exposure to daily life in a busy household, if they are to make good pets in their new homes.

7–12 weeks

Most kittens go to their new homes between the ages of eight and ten weeks. Occasionally, the owner decides that they cannot bear to part with any kittens that their queen has had and keeps the entire litter. The success or failure of this decision depends on several different factors.

In a wild situation, natural dispersion of a litter of kittens would be inevitable. There are few places in the world where natural resources, such as prey animals or den sites, are so abundant that all the animals in a

left *Getting to know you: Kittens are extremely curious.*

litter could be fed and sheltered in one area. In our domestic homes, it is possible to provide enough food, resting places, toys, and affection for several cats to live together... but how harmonious this situation is depends on the collective personalities of the various pets!

For most kittens, leaving their mother and littermates is therefore a natural progression and not a wrench or an emotional parting. Kittens usually adjust very quickly to the surroundings of their new home, and after some initial caution, blossom as the only cat to receive all the family's attention.

As soon as they arrive, most kittens start to mark their new home as their territory. This is usually done through cheek-rubbing of furniture, walls, and even people. Some kittens may become a little confused and try to mark more rigorously, either by scratching or using urine or feces, but such cases are relatively rare (see pages 104–105).

Until your kitten can go outside after his vaccinations, the interior of

your home is his entire world. The chances are that he will love exploring, and open doors, cupboards, and even carryalls and sports bags will seem like enticing new places in which to venture. This short period of habituation is usually a delight for owners and kittens alike. Although having a young kitten around can be hard work, it is absolutely fascinating to watch their antics as they learn about the world.

sharpening hunter skills

Physically, your kitten is likely to be able to execute all the skills of an adult, although probably not to perfection! Stalking and pouncing, particularly, are practiced at this time, as kittens learn to judge speed and distance—important factors for expert hunting.

Kittens often adopt an unusual stance when stalking "prey," with the front end crouched low and the back feet treading alternately on the spot. No one really knows why this posture is taken up during stalking,

above *A new home offers the chance of physical and behavioral development.*

although it may assist in coordination or helps kittens and cats to accurately gauge the distance between their targets and themselves.

Continued socialization and habituation is vital during this last section of the critical period. Kittens continue to learn about how to react to stimuli, making the introduction of many people visiting the house very important. Once in a new home, kittens need to learn the family's routine and habits. Human beings must be very surprising to them—we take showers, sneeze, shout, laugh, and talk to plastic machines that make surprising ringing sounds. A kitten who has already developed confidence and curiosity in the activities going on around him will have no problem adjusting to such experiences; others, however, may take a little longer.

3–6 months

The period between three and six months is another milestone in your kitten's development. Kittens of this age range are generally building their independence. In the wild, littermates disperse during this time, to find their own hunting grounds, den sites, and eventually a mate. In our domestic environment, this is reflected in the kittens' desire to wander further afield.

Territory-marking through scratching, urine, and feces starts now, and competition between neighboring cats, or even cats in the same home, may develop.

Adult teeth are established before the age of six months and solid food is fully accepted. At the same time, production of the enzyme that helps to digest milk rapidly diminishes, making it more difficult for milk to be tolerated.

Sexual development is not usually complete until six months of age, but the use of the feline's special vomeronasal organ starts to come into play. Known as Jacobson's organ, it is located in the roof of the mouth, directly above the upper incisors. Two fluid-filled sacs are connected to the nasal cavity by ducts that transmit scent particles. This organ allows the particles to be tasted and smelled at the same time, giving greatly heightened scent awareness and examination of odors.

taste and the Flehmen response

The Jacobson's organ is used in connection with sexual behavior. Male cats often draw in the smell of females' urine or scent gland secretions over the vomeronasal organ to "taste" it. This action sometimes creates an intense look of concentration in the cat,

left *Cats hone their hunting skills during adolescence.*

combined with a distinctive mouth posture, as the lips are drawn back. The cat's teeth may chatter together as he analyzes the smell, and salivation sometimes occurs. This characteristic behavior is called the Flehmen response. It is thought to be an integral part of judging sexual response in the opposite sex, but is also seen in response to the sight of prey.

During this teenage like stage of life, kittens are likely to "test" their owners to see what their responses will be. Many kittens of this age start to be fussy with food and experiment to see what is offered if they refuse their usual diet. At this point, many owners embark on a lifetime of slavery, as their wily cat sends them off to the store to buy different food almost every day!

Cats also try different means of communication at this age. Discovering that vocalizations usually result in human responses, many cats learn an impressive range of calls, chirrups, and meows to let their owners know what they want. Unfortunately, some are so good at this that yowling at 3am becomes the norm!

Just like human teenagers, kittens need to know where they stand if they are not to become overly demanding. However, punishment is never an appropriate option to teaching good behavior. Instead, understanding why your cat does what he or she does is always the first step to resolving any conflicts.

6–12 months

By this stage your kitten is physically a fully fledged cat. Sexual development is normally complete by the age of six months, which means that neutering needs to be done prior to this to be certain of unwanted litters of new kittens.

Your young cat will be able to behave like his parents, grandparents, and ancestors before him. Running, climbing, stalking, and pouncing will all be expertly practiced and your cat may start to bring you "gifts" of prey that he has killed, given the opportunity.

How much your cat hunts depends upon a number of factors. Early maternal teaching has some influence, as kittens that have the chance to copy their mother get off to a flying start.

However, the environment in which your cat now lives also has a bearing. Urbanized areas have different types of prey than in the countryside. Birds and

below *Alert and ready for action, this tabby shows her wild side.*

rats are the most common quarry of city-dwelling cats and are more difficult to catch than other types of prey—and less rewarding, since rats are notoriously unappetizing and rarely consumed! In the countryside, mice and other wild rodents are more commonly caught, although some country-dwelling cats become expert at taking larger prey, particularly rabbits.

The density of the local cat population has an influence on how often and how far afield your pet goes hunting. The range of a neutered male cat can be a mile in diameter, and even more in some cases, but some routes may be treacherous to cross. Traffic and the territories of other felines may persuade some cats that lying at the fireside is safer than hunting!

lap cats and watcher cats

Adult cats are usually excellent routine-watchers. In only a matter of days, they can predict our routines and habits—and capitalize on them! In most households, the cat is fed, groomed, played with, and petted according to relatively fixed time ranges. School hours, work routines, and bedtimes are all closely observed by cats, who start to match them with their own internal body-clock.

As a species, felines are crepuscular—they are most active at dawn and dusk. This fits the lifestyle of most families quite well, as cats are at their most interactive in the morning and evening, before and after people are at work or school. In between, cats are usually more than happy to sleep and conserve energy, for anything up to six hours at a time.

This behavior does not mean that cats do not need or appreciate company and social contact. By adulthood, a cat's personality is formed, and most domestic animals fall into two distinct categories: lap cats and watchers.

Lap cats just love to be stroked and cuddled. They will sit on your lap as soon as you sit down and often refuse to move, clinging on until the last second when you need to get up. These cats are usually very demonstrative and demanding; physical contact means everything to them and they will work hard to get it.

The other type of cat is just as affectionate and loving, but does not enjoy being restrained in any way—watchers. These cats do not choose to sit on laps; instead they often prefer to sit beside you on the couch and watch TV. Moves toward them or any commotion usually drives them away. Such cats are often more independent characters who love to have people nearby but prefer to watch rather then interact.

Both sets of characteristics are rewarding, in their own way. Whichever personality your kitten develops, enjoy it!

socialization in the critical period

Cats are truly amazing creatures. As descendants and close relatives of the wild cats that still populate many areas of the globe, they are driven by basic instinct, yet as our pets, living in our homes, they are able to show a domesticated side to their nature that makes them affectionate and endearing. These two sides to the cat are both born and made.

Genetic information is passed from mother and father to each kitten, and this ensures that the kitten grows up to hunt, stalk, chase, and even kill small prey, if it has the opportunity. On the other hand, learning and particularly early socialization means that cats gradually discover how to relate to people, other cats, and even other species of animal living in the same household. Learning to interact with their own and other species is called socialization, and studies have proven that this needs to take place during a particular period of the kitten's life.

This critical period, or sensitive period as it is sometimes known, takes place between the ages of two and seven weeks. During this time kittens must meet and be handled by as many different people as possible. Handling by only one or two people may reduce the risks of infection, but greatly increases the risk of fear, anxiety, and stress-related problems later in life.

People of all types, ages, and appearances need to become familiar to kittens during the critical period.

left *This kitten's posture shows she is enjoying social interaction with her owner.*

From a human viewpoint, most people look roughly the same; however, to a kitten certain individuals can look like another species altogether! For example, your kitten may have become perfectly comfortable with being handled by a particular man, but the same man wearing a hat or glasses could seem completely different.

sounds and movements
Kittens need to learn about human communication in the critical period. People show their teeth when they smile, use their hands to communicate, make strange noises when speaking, and behave unexpectedly—by clapping or sneezing, for example.

Between two and seven weeks of age, kittens need to understand that different people smell different, too. This may not be as obvious to us—the human sense of smell is poor compared to that of cats, so scent may be overlooked. Deodorant, perfume, exhaust fumes, detergent, cigarette smoke, and even human perspiration need to become familiar to your kitten if he or she is not to be afraid of these types of odors later on.

For some kittens, it is important that they learn how to interrelate with members of their own species, and other species, too. Cats are designed to be solitary hunters and live alone. However, with adequate time spent playing and communicating with other cats, kittens learn to get along with them extremely well.

Learning feline body language and facial expressions is a vital part of this socialization phase, and also needs to occur before seven weeks of age. This is particularly relevant for hand-reared kittens or singletons, which may miss out on their mother's lessons in communication or the chance to play with other kittens. Similarly, the chance to grow up with a friendly dog or even a horse during this period ensures that such animals are regarded as part of the family, not a threat.

habituation

A kitten growing up in a domestic situation has a very different life to that of his wild ancestor. Our pets have to learn to cope with all the sights, sounds, smells, and sensations of our modern existence, and they need to become familiar early in life if they are to cope as an adult.

Kittens under the age of about 12 weeks seem to know little fear. Most are outgoing, curious, and keen to explore. This is the time to make sure that they are totally familiar with household objects, sounds, and experiences. Some supervision and safety measures are obviously required, but try not to shelter your kitten too much. Experiencing the world in the home and at large is all part of growing up.

sights

From a kitten's point of view, some aspects of our environment must look very strange. Imagine meeting a vacuum cleaner for the first time, or a person wearing a hat. It is unsurprising that some kittens choose to run away when they first see odd sights. It takes time for them to understand that the everyday elements of human life that we take for granted do not represent danger and that they can safely be ignored.

sounds

Cats have extremely good hearing so even relatively soft sounds must seem loud and intrusive to them. All kittens need to learn that sounds created by the washing machine on fast spin, the microwave oven, or even children playing are non-threatening and simply part of life.

smells

Familiarizing your kitten with the smell of many different people is vital. Cats have a highly acute sense of smell—it is so powerful that cats tend to use it to recognize each other—and us—rather than identifying living things by sight. Many different people need to handle your kitten and teach him or her that it is pleasurable to be touched and to have close contact with beings who smell different from each other.

touch

All cats need to learn that being touched is pleasant, not frightening. Veterinary examination, veterinary treatment, and grooming all require extensive handling, while strokes and cuddles become part of a close and loving relationship. Although it is perfectly acceptable for your pet to be a

left *Gentle but thorough examination prepares the kitten for veterinary treatment.*

watcher rather than a lap cat, he should not be fearful of human contact.

familiarizing your kitten

Make sure that you get your kitten as early as possible. The true socialization phase in kittens' development finishes at seven weeks, and by 12 weeks many behavior patterns and responses may be fixed.

Invite as many people to your home as possible to meet your kitten, and make sure that greeting them is pleasurable for your kitten, by providing food treats and stroking. It is also essential that your pet has the opportunity to hear ordinary domestic sounds and see domestic life in all their glory. Do not be over-protective and shelter your kitten

above *This stunning Bengal demonstrates his climbing and balancing abilities.*

from noises or things that are new to him, but allow him to investigate them. Ignore all fear responses and encourage brave behavior by praising and stroking your kitten when he is being adventurous.

weaning: its behavioral importance

From the moment of birth until kittens are about three weeks old, they depend entirely on their mother's milk to survive. The queen feeds her kittens almost on demand, only leaving the nest to relieve herself and to go on hunting or feeding expeditions for herself. But this can't go on forever and how the young are made to move on to solid food is a vital part of their emotional development.

At around three weeks of age, kittens start to become much more mobile and active. This is the start of their transition from dependent beings to solitary and independent hunters. At this stage, their mother starts to spend longer periods away from them. On her return, the kittens swamp her, demanding to feed and barging each other to be first in line.

Feeding so many hungry mouths is obviously very draining on the queen. Indeed, it would be impossible for her to maintain the kittens' growth rate without serious consequences to her own health, and hence weaning onto solid foods—and learning hunting skills—must start.

The weaning process is not only physically important, but emotionally and behaviorally, too. In a wild situation, the mother begins to return from hunts with prey that she has already caught, either dead or stunned. She drops the prey in the nest and encourages the kittens to look toward this new type of food, rather than relying on her milk supply.

coping with frustration

This transition is a difficult one for the kittens. Their only experience of food so far has been her milk, and they usually try to get to her teats whenever they are hungry. In order to stop the suckling response and focus the kittens' attention on prey instead, the mother has to make her disapproval clear whenever kittens attempt to feed from her.

right *Play is an essential part of learning hunting skills.*

below *It takes time and a little practice to learn to eat solid food.*

To begin with, she is likely to simply stand up and walk away. The kittens drop off her teats in a very undignified manner, but they aren't immediately discouraged. Each attempt to reach the mother's milk is met with in the same way: rejection. This is the first time that the kittens have had to learn to cope with frustration—they can see what they want but cannot have it.

This frustration eventually leads the kittens to try a different tactic and they have to take note of the meals that the mother has brought back to the nest—or in a domestic situation, the bowls of food that have been provided by the breeder. At this point, kittens learn that the arrival of their mother, or their substitute mother in the shape of a human, is a prelude to the arrival of solid food and they stop trying to gain access to their mother's milk.

Weaning is the kittens' first lesson in how to resolve conflict. There will be many other conflicts in their lives and it is vital that kittens know how to cope with them. Without such early lessons, kittens can grow into cats that do not know how to deal with frustration and may use aggression in an attempt to get what they want instead. Indeed, hand-reared kittens that have not been subjected to this behavioral process often display such inappropriate behavior.

right *Weaning begins when the queen walks away from her kittens while they are feeding.*

social communication

Cats are not designed to live together. They do not form social groups in the same way that dogs do, and they hunt independently. However, this does not mean that cats do not communicate with each other.

Cat communication is rich and complex, although it is very different from that of a truly social species, which communicate up close. Cats have relatively few facial expressions and even their vocalization is more limited than a social species, such as the dog. Instead, they use signals which can be read and understood at a distance. Body language is sometimes used—anyone who has ever seen a cat arch its back, fluff up its tail, and hiss and spit will attest to that!—but common forms of feline communication are more subtle.

below *The sense of smell is vital to cats.*

scent in feline communication

If humans can be said to live in a world of sight and sound, cats surely live in a world of scent. This is the feline's major sense; although their sight and hearing are also excellent, cats can "read" smells over vast distances and with great accuracy.

Since humans have such a poor sense of smell, compared with cats, this aspect of their abilities is little understood. We know that cats use and respond to scent to communicate with each other. This is primarily because cats are not a social species so much communication is done at a distance.

For example, in the wild a cat would probably only meet up with another in order to mate. To attract a mate, both male and female need to leave "air-mail" scent messages to let others know that they are in the area. Once they have mated, the pair will have little to do with one another and instead use scent messages to avoid meeting again if one needs to cross the other's territory.

Scents are left in the form of cheek gland secretions, urine marks, and feces, which are deliberately left uncovered so that they are highly noticeable. Cats also scratch trees and posts to leave both a visual mark and a scent message, using secretions from between their foot pads.

Domestic cats have developed to tolerate the close proximity of other cats in their areas, but they use scent messages in the same ways as their wild cousins. It is not surprising that the majority of behavioral problems in cats involve urine and feces in the home, placed there quite deliberately by an animal who is trying to communicate, but is misunderstood and unappreciated by humans.

Domestic cats have four main ways of using scent communication, as follows.

rubbing

Cheek glands, which run from the corner of the cat's mouth to the outer corner of the eye, produce pheromone

right *Cats spread the "clan odor" by rubbing their scent onto members of the family.*

substances that are individual to each and every cat. This is like a fingerprint; although some of the chemical constituents are the same in all cats, the others are unique.

Cats use pheromones to increase their feelings of security. They rub us, other animals that they feel comfortable with, and even furniture in order to make these things smell the same as they do. Cats living together rub, wash, and groom each other so that their scent becomes shared and they build up what is known as a "clan odor." If we have been out all day, or have been walking around outside, we come home and smell very different from our cats. They then feel the need to "replenish" their smell on us, and so rub their heads and bodies on us to restore the "family" smell.

The chemical constituents of the cheek glands break down over a period of time, so cats need to refresh the smell around them at least once or twice a day in order to maintain their security. Secure cats who are content in their own environment rub people, furniture, and other animals frequently and expressively, and this is to be encouraged.

scratching

Scratching also leaves scent on the area being marked. Cats have scent glands between the pads of the feet so scratching leaves both a visual mark and a scent mark at the same time. Scratching usually means that the cat is feeling a little anxious and needs to make himself feel more secure by marking his area. Nearly all cats scratch outside, if permitted. This is perfectly acceptable. Indoors, cats need a scratching post to keep their claws in good condition, but scratching other areas may indicate stress.

urine

The majority of cats, male and female, neutered or not, spray urine to mark outside. This is perfectly normal—the cat is simply marking territory, leaving information for other cats in the area to "read." This probably tells cats who sprayed the urine, how long ago, and even how fit they are.

Spraying urine involves the cat backing up to an upright object, lifting the tail up high, and squirting urine as high as possible up a tree or post. Many cats also perform a characteristic padding motion with their back feet while spraying.

The chemical constituents of urine break down over a period of time, so cats usually re-mark territory at least once a day. Cats who spray urine in the home are usually showing anxiety. Finding the cause of the stress is essential if you are to stop this behavior (see page 104).

feces

Feces are a very obvious message, as left uncovered they offer clear visual impact, as well as odor! Cats often defecate outdoors in obvious places where territories overlap—the feces mark boundaries of territory, as well as carrying information about the cat. This behavior is known as middening.

Unfortunately, some kittens and cats also use middening indoors. This can be to reduce anxiety or make themselves feel more secure. Middening is often a feline attempt to link their smell as closely as possible with that of their owner—and often they choose to defecate in the middle of their owner's bed or in his or her shoes (see page 102).

below *Males and females both spray outdoors to mark territory.*

communicating
with cats

When you want to communicate with your kitten, you need to be close to him or her—humans can't communicate with scent markings! It is essential that you learn to "talk cat" and can recognize feline facial expressions and body language.

right *Face to face—learning social communication.*

eyes

A cat's eyes are very expressive. Narrowing the eyes or widening them can indicate the mood that the animal is in, and the pupils also give an indication of feeling.

A relaxed cat will probably have half-closed or heavy eyelids. A cat that is really contented often blinks slowly and turns their face away from the person that they are communicating with. If you copy this behavior, by turning your face away, half-closing your eyes and blinking, you may find that you get into a real "conversation" with your kitten, where you each take turns to show this behavior.

A fearful cat usually has dilated pupils and opens its eyes as wide as possible. An aggressive or angry cat may also have its eyes wide open, but the pupils are constricted to a thin slit. Of course, the amount of light available also influences pupil dilation.

ears

Cats' ears have an incredible range of movement, both for locating sounds and to show

emotion. Up to 30 muscles control these movements and mean that cat ears can flatten toward the head, prick in interest, swivel through 180 degrees, and move independently of one another.

A relaxed cat usually holds its ears facing forward and angled back slightly. If the cat becomes more aroused, the ears angle forward to show interest. Fearful cats tend to flatten their ears in an attempt to make their whole outline look smaller, while aggressive cats swivel their ears around so that the insides of the flaps face the sides and the backs are shown.

tail

The sight of a cat running toward its owner with its tail held high in greeting is a perfect image of cat/human communication. The tail is often kinked over slightly at the top, which is an invitation to explore the animal's main scent regions under the tail.

Relaxed cats usually let their tails hang down. Fearful cats or those who are becoming aroused, active, or annoyed may swish their tails gently from side to side. A tail thrashed vigorously from side to side in a whip-like motion indicates high excitement or aggression.

Kittens often play by running crazily around in a random pattern. While doing so their tails are usually carried in an inverted "U" shape that shows their sense of fun.

rubbing

All cats use scent to communicate (see page 30). Rubbing can be used to ask for food or attention and to make sure all the family smell the same. Relaxed, contented cats rub like this a lot, which shows good communication in the household.

purring and meowing

Nearly all kittens and cats purr when they are content. How exactly this sound is generated we still do not know, but kittens purr from an early age, particularly when suckling, to

above *Many cats learn to enjoy close contact with their owners.*

show their pleasure. When kittens move to their new homes, we take on the maternal role, which is perhaps why the purring continues.

However, purring is not always a sign of happiness. Cats are sometimes reported to purr even when in extreme pain after accidents, or when being given veterinary treatment after surgery. This implies that purring may also represent some sort of social submission signal.

Some cats meow more than others. This may be due to the breed— Siamese are the most talkative—or to the individual cat's experiences. For example, many cats learn that meowing results in their owner talking to them, calling out to them, or feeding them. Repeating this behavior is then a good example of how cats train humans!

which kitten for me?

The decision to get any kind of pet should be taken with due consideration to time, space, and money. Cats are no exception. Despite their reputation as independent creatures, cats need feeding, cleaning, grooming, veterinary care and treatment, training, and company. Sadly, rescue centers across the globe are full of unwanted cats, the majority of which started out life as a much-loved kitten in a family home. Even more cats live a stray or feral existence, never having had the comforts and luxuries of a home to live in or a supply of food they can rely upon.

Before embarking on a relationship that should grow and develop over 15 to 20 years, you should be certain that you know all the needs and demands that a kitten will have and be able to meet them. Children particularly are eager and interested in animals when they are small and cute, but litter boxes still need cleaning and feeding still costs money when the kitten grows into a cat and the novelty wears off.

Due consideration to the environment is vital if you are planning to get a kitten. All kittens need to be kept indoors until their vaccinations are complete. However, when they can go outside, how safe is your local environment for a cat by itself? Many cats are killed in road traffic accidents each year, many stray away from home, and many incur injuries as a result of other accidents.

If you live near a busy highway or fear for a cat in other ways, fencing your yard or keeping your pet permanently indoors may be the only truly safe options. These lifestyles too have implications, for your time and money and for the kitten's future welfare and behavior.

making the commitment

Sadly, many cats are given drugs, needlessly declawed, or are even euthanized, just because they behave like cats. Keeping a cat indoors will not stem his or her desire to hunt, climb, chase, and pounce, so these behaviors need an appropriate outlet if they are not to become a problem. Are you prepared to invest the time, money, and effort needed to ensure that your pet is happy and content for its entire life?

left *Natural instincts at work.*

Keeping cats offers many benefits to human beings. Research has shown that stroking cats can reduce blood pressure and heart rate. Families who keep animals and interact positively with them are likely to suffer fewer minor illnesses, such as colds, viruses, and headaches. Animals have also been shown to increase communication and interaction in families—they offer a common social denominator that allows people to talk together and focus on another individual that requires effort to maintain and manage.

However, we have to remember that while cats are good for us, we also need to be good for them. If you suspect that taking on a kitten will only add to your current burden of

above *Kittens kept indoors need stimulation if behavior problems are to be prevented.*

family commitments, work demands, time constraints, and financial pressures, wait before purchasing a kitten. An animal can only enhance the positive aspects of your life—it cannot solve your problems!

breed and gender

pedigree kittens

A pedigree kitten is one born from a litter where both parents were of the same pedigree breed. This means that the eventual size, appearance, and behavioral characteristics of your kitten in adulthood will be predictable.

Other aspects are also predictable: some pedigree breeds suffer from inherited diseases and even behavioral

problems that can be passed from parents to offspring. For example, Oriental cats seem far more prone to wool-eating problems than other breeds. Persians are more likely to suffer from house-training problems than other types of cat.

crossbreed kittens

Cross-bred kittens come from a litter where the queen was one pedigree breed and the tom was another pedigree breed. Such kittens often combine the

qualities of both parents extremely well, but they may look or behave more like one parent than the other.

mixed-breed kittens

Mixed-bred kittens are exactly that! Affectionately known by some as "moggies," these animals make up around 90 percent of the world's cat population. These are cats whose parentage is completely unknown. Their eventual appearance and characteristics are difficult to predict, although their

below *Male (left) and female kittens.*

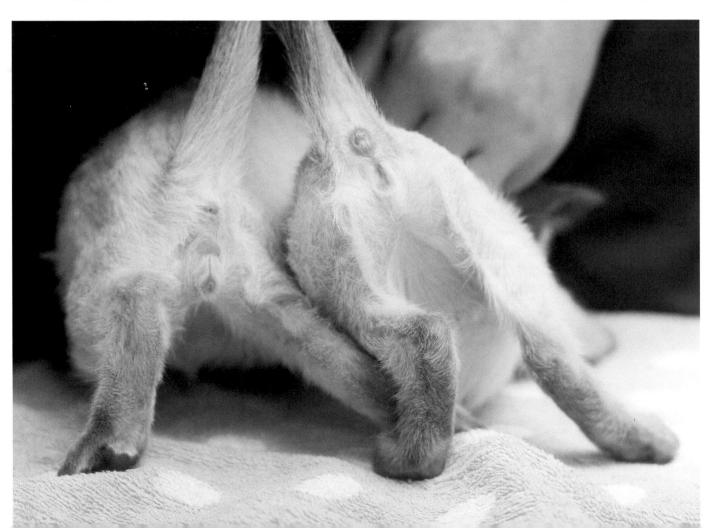

above *These sisters are likely to remain close companions.*

size is usually consistent with the size of their mother and father.

Mixed-breed cats do not tend to suffer from inherited diseases in the same way that pedigree animals do. Although they are more robust in that way, they are just as susceptible to infections and other diseases.

which gender?

Choosing which gender of kitten to buy is a matter of personal preference. There is some evidence that males are more competitive and potentially more aggressive to other cats than females, but these drives are generally reduced

dramatically by neutering. Equally, the most common cause of anxiety for owners of female kittens is that their pet will become pregnant and produce an unwanted litter. Neutering before the age of six months obviously prevents this also.

Perhaps the only time when choosing which sex to buy really matters is when introducing a kitten to an older, established cat in the household. In this instance, buying the opposite sex seems to offer the best chance of a successful relationship forming between them.

Sexing kittens is notoriously difficult. Many owners are surprised to be told

on the first visit to the veterinarian that all is not as they originally presumed and Tigger needs to be renamed Tabitha! In the male kitten, the penis is well hidden, and is only discernible by looking for a small opening approximately two-fifths of an inch below the anus. The female's vulva is seen as a vertical slit, which appears to be almost joined to the anus. Ask your veterinarian to confirm the sex of your kitten if you are unsure.

age and number of kittens

your kitten's age

Unfortunately, the age at which you can purchase a pedigree kitten may be out of your control. In many countries, cat pedigree organizations regulate the registration and sale of kittens. The feline equivalent of the Kennel Club, they include the American Cat Fanciers' Association, International Cat Association, Governing Council of the Cat Fancy (UK), and other European equivalents. They precludes sales of pedigree animals before the age of 12 weeks, by which time the kittens should be fully vaccinated and litter-trained.

Provided the kitten has encountered as many different people and experiences as possible by 12 weeks, there should be no problem. However, this is well beyond the critical socialization phase, which ends at seven weeks, and can mean that the kitten's whole outlook on life is fixed by the time he or she arrives in your home. A kitten from an under-stimulating or deprived background can have problems for life.

Most mixed-breed kittens are able to leave their mother and littermates at eight weeks, and this is an ideal time to bring him or her home. Of course, you will still need to build on your kitten's social experiences and complete his or her vaccination program after this time.

how many kittens?

Although cats are not a truly social species, they can and do enjoy each other's company, particularly if two kittens are raised together from one litter. Brothers and sisters can form close bonds, and their interactions and relationships can be highly rewarding—for them and their owner.

A single kitten in a household is entirely dependent upon all the family members for social contact and company. Games and play times need to be increased to strengthen the relationships between humans and kitten, especially if the pet is slightly nervous or under-socialized.

Of course, two kittens have each other to play with. This reduces the

right Bonding with the human family is particularly important for the single cat.

left Kittens of similar age bond well if brought up together, particularly if they are siblings.

amount of time that you need to devote to playing games and giving affection. It also offers the most wonderful opportunity to watch feline behavior at work, as the kittens run and play together, use body signaling, and show affection for each other.

However, it also means that the kittens may bond with each other just as closely as they will to you, and may even rely on each other more than their owner. This does not usually present a problem unless one of the kittens is lost, or until one of the pets dies. This can leave the remaining cat utterly bereft; research has shown that they seem to grieve over their loss, as we do.

Choosing kittens from the same litter is usually ideal if you plan to have a pair. Two kittens from different litters need to be relatively

close in age if they are to readily accept each other, and both need to be clear of any infections or parasites that could be transferred from one to the other.

Later in life, males are generally more competitive than females. This means that one male and one female, or two females, are usually the best choices to live permanently together.

when to buy a kitten

Bear in mind that nature has designed cats to reproduce during spring and summer, when there is plenty of prey around to sustain a growing family in the wild. Domestic cats seem to have retained this original programming and are much more likely to produce kittens during these seasons, which may make it harder to find a litter if buying during cooler months.

choosing a pedigree kitten

Unlike dogs, which show more diversity than most species on the planet, cats follow their original blueprint almost to the letter. Over the centuries, man's interference has made very little difference to the shape of the cat. Color and coat length are the only two significant changes that selective breeding has consistently produced; although anomalies occur, allowing the shape of the ears or tail to look different, such breeds are few and far between. Because of this, cat breeds are categorized by coat length into three main groups: shorthairs, semi-longhairs, and longhairs.

shorthairs

Although the vast majority of domestic cats are shorthairs, they tend to be non-pedigrees. However, several pedigree shorthair types do exist:

Siamese

Perhaps the most recognizable of all the shorthairs, the Siamese is as distinctive in character as it is in looks. These cats are slender, elegant, and sinuous. Their long legs and long, thin tails add to the svelte outline. Even the Siamese's head is long, and wedge-shaped—almost triangular. The profile from head to nose is a straight line, and huge almond-shaped eyes slant toward the nose. Siamese come in a range of different color markings. The

below *Sealpoint Siamese kittens.*

above *A magnificent blue Burmese.*

most common is seal-point, but chocolate, lilac, red, cream, tortoiseshell, and tabby are among other colors allowed by cat fancier groups. All Siamese have clear blue eyes, which start out baby blue, and reach their final piercing hue at around eight weeks of age.

Siamese are huge personalities in a slender frame. They can domineer their owners, and often other pets. Intelligent and trainable, they can learn to walk on a harness and leash and enjoy walks with their owners. These are cats for those who love communication! Siamese are known for their insistent and demanding cries, howls, and mews. They are not cats to be ignored!

Burmese

Now a very popular pet, the Burmese has built a real following in the USA and Europe. These cats are medium in size, with rounded heads and wide-set ears. Their eyes are large and intelligent. The muzzle is shorter than the Siamese's, with a pronounced chin and a strong jaw. The coat is short, dense, and so glossy that these cats look almost polished! Brown and sable are the colors most recognized by cat fanciers' groups, but all are recognized somewhere around the world.

These are graceful, elegant cats, with a great sense of humor. Almost dog-like in behavior, Burmese are prone to behavioral problems simply because their intelligence and need for stimulation are often overlooked.

Abyssinian

Perhaps the most striking aspect of this lion-like cat is its double-ticked coat.

right *The double-ticked coat of the Abyssinian.*

Each golden hair is striped by dark brown, giving a textured appearance. Abyssinians have slightly triangular faces, with huge eyes of green, hazel, or yellow. This is a slender cat, with a long graceful tail. The whole appearance is one of strength and elegance combined.

Abyssinians seem to attach themselves closely to their owners. However, they are also outgoing and friendly, and get along well with children and dogs. They are an intelligent breed and can usually be taught to retrieve.

American Shorthair/ British Shorthair

The American Shorthair is a large and sturdy animal weighing around 14 pounds, with a big, round head and large eyes. These popular cats can be any color, from solid black through to spotted and tortoiseshell. Their British cousins, the British Shorthair, have smaller heads.

These "square" cats are known to be excellent family pets, good with children and happy to sit on anyone's lap.

Korat

This striking cat is always a fabulous silver-blue. The name is pronounced "koh-raht" and reflects its Thai ancestry, where the cat was regarded as so precious that it could only be given as a gift from one owner to another. The Korat has a distinctive heart-shaped face, large luminous green eyes, and a graceful body.

In general, these cats are gentle, quiet, and intelligent. They can be anxious about strangers in the home and males particularly are reputed to be intolerant of other cats. More than most breeds, Korats should be carefully selected from a breeder whose first priorities are sound temperaments and early socialization.

Manx

This is one of the few breeds that is immediately recognizable to any cat lover, as it has no tail. The Manx is officially recognized in several versions: the tailless Rumpy, the Rumpy-riser—which has a few tail vertebrae—the short-tailed Stumpy,

above *Korats have a characteristic heart-shaped face.*

and the Tailed, which has an almost full-length tail. Only true Rumpies are considered for showing. This strange anomaly is the result of a genetic fault, so it is vital to breed the varieties together to keep the resulting offspring strong and healthy in other ways. All colors are allowed.

The Manx is known for its friendliness and hunting prowess.

semi-longhairs
Birman

This beautiful cat is medium-to-large in size, with a large round head, a straight nose, a long body, and strong legs and paws. The body hair is long, silky, and golden. The "points"—eye mask, ears, legs, and tail—may be in a darker color. The eyes are round and bright blue, with a depth and clarity that is almost startling.

Birmans are known to be friendly and affectionate. Their coats are relatively easy to care for.

Balinese

This cat is a close relative of the Siamese, but has a semi-long coat, which is fine and silky in texture and easily groomed, as it doesn't mat. The cat's body is elegant and slender; their movement is so graceful that the breed is named after Balinese dancers, famed for their flowing movements.

These cats are lively, but not as noisy as their full Siamese cousins.

Maine Coon

This cat has recently become fashionable—and the cost of Maine Coon kittens reflects this! Males may be up to 18lb in weight and both genders are sturdy and robust, with a thick weatherproof coat. The tail is

above *The open expression of a Ragdoll kitten.*

left *A handsome Maine Coon and its heavily plumed tail.*

usually a magnificent plume, which perhaps added to the legend that this breed was created by matings between a cat and a raccoon, hence the name.

Maine Coons are confident, outgoing, and energetic. They need plenty of activity to prevent them becoming "self-employed" and finding their own, perhaps undesirable ways to amuse themselves.

Ragdoll

This is an exceptional cat, showing the extent to which genetics have been manipulated by man. Large and heavy, with a flat-skulled head and wedge-shaped face, the blue eyes are large and oval, with an open expression oozing with charm.

However, it is the personality and behavior of Ragdoll cats that makes them special. Not only are they placid and biddable, but they become "ragdoll-like" when picked up and held. Indeed, these cats can become so floppy that they feel almost bendable! This characteristic has led to some owners being concerned about their Ragdoll's ability to defend itself out of doors, and many are therefore kept as house pets.

Norwegian Forest Cat

A real outdoor type from Scandinavia, the Norwegian Forest Cat has a thick weatherproof coat that has a double layer to protect against the cold.

Muscular and powerful, these cats are renowned for their hunting and climbing abilities. Indeed, they are reputed to be able to climb rocks as well as trees! Affectionate, intelligent, and active, examples of this breed do not appreciate being confined indoors.

Somali

The Somali is really a semi-longhaired Abyssinian. They have heavily tufted ears, a thick fox-like tail, and an athletic outline.

These cats need outdoor activities and exercise, as well as a devoted family. They are generally friendly and extrovert.

Turkish Van

Named after the Lake Van region of Turkey, where this breed was first discovered, the Turkish Van has one striking behavioral characteristic that sets it apart from other cats: it loves water! These cats like to swim, paddle, and drink water; owners tell tales of their cats joining them in the bath, drinking from the faucet, and diving into the lavatory!

The coat is silky in texture, and is white with auburn markings on the face and tail.

longhairs
Persian

The Persian is probably the world's most well-recognized breed of cat. Flat faced and with a long, luxuriant coat, these cats have been popular since they were first shown as a pure breed in the late 19th century. Persians have short legs and stocky bodies, which can make them less active than other types of cat. Their coat

left *The distinctive Persian.*

requires considerable daily grooming if it is not to knot and tangle, and the eye area often needs to be cleaned manually to prevent tear-staining.

Gentle and friendly, Persians have many fans across the globe who are prepared to maintain the coat in order to have the benefits of this affectionate character.

other coats

Rex

Both the Cornish and Devon Rex cats are known for their curly, rather sparse coats. They have large eyes and ears and whip-like tails. Rexes have been bred from naturally occurring mutations in normal litters of kittens, and come in a range of colors. They may be suitable for those who are

allergic to other cat hair—the texture and the reduction in molting can make them more acceptable.

Playful, friendly, and "talkative," these cats are for the owner looking for something special.

above Rex breeds, like this Cornish example, have unusually textured fur.

Sphynx

This cat is as hairless as they get! A soft down lightly covers the skin, clearly revealing the skin's own patterns, colors, and wrinkles. This cat needs skin protection in hot weather and additional warmth in the cold. It also needs more frequent feeding than other breeds, as it stores very little fat.

This breed is not widely recognized but has its fans across the world. It is said to be sweet-natured and gentle.

left The fur pattern a Sphynx would display is shown in its skin markings.

where to get your kitten

Traditionally, obtaining a kitten was more by default than design. If a neighbor's cat accidentally had kittens, the owner was more than grateful to ensure that each kitten had a good home and usually gave them away to friends and family. In these days of increased neutering and the control of strays, however, you will probably have to decide where to get your kitten.

Be wary of pet stores. While such places are ideal for buying all the accoutrements that your kitten will need, stores are not the best place to find a kitten. You cannot see the mother with her kittens—and since the first two to seven weeks of your kitten's life may determine his or her behavior and personality for the next 15 to 20 years, background and parentage is vitally important.

Some kittens bought from stores were taken from their mother and littermates too early, reducing the kitten's ability to communicate with his own species and increasing the chance of litter training problems. Illnesses and parasites are more common among live pet shop stock, primarily because so many animals are brought together under one roof, despite the cleanest surroundings.

below *A domestic setting offers kittens an ideal start, with opportunity for early socialization*

breeder

If you want a pedigree kitten, you need to find one from a reputable breeder. Organizations such as the American Cat Fanciers' Association, International Cat Association (USA), and the Governing Council of the Cat Fancy in the UK have lists of breeders who specialize in each breed, and will help prospective owners to get in touch with them. Other countries have similar organizations, so ask your veterinarian to help you get in contact with one.

It is very important that you visit the breeder, view the conditions in

which the kittens have been kept, and see the mother. If you can see the father too, so much the better, as kittens often seem to inherit his sociability (see page 55).

The kittens are most likely to be kept in an outdoor cattery pen with their mother. This should be clean and tidy, but without being sparse or non-stimulating. Indeed, the ideal breeder needs to understand the balance between cleanliness and a socially challenging environment and provide a compromise between them.

Most breeders are extremely careful about where their kittens are homed. A

above *Pure-bred kittens should be obtained from a reputable breeder.*

conscientious breeder will ask lots of questions about your lifestyle, what you know about the breed, and your home and yard—not just how you would like to pay.

neighbor

This is still the ideal place to obtain a mixed-breed kitten. Kittens that have been brought up in the heart of the family with their mother are already likely to be confident around children, the domestic environment, and all the sights and sounds of an average home. If the mother is a relaxed and contented individual, it's likely the kittens will have similar temperaments, too.

Of course, many such kittens are born without the owner of the queen ever knowing who the father was. Bear in mind that the father's genetic influence is just as strong as the mother's, and that this part of your kitten's personality may not be immediately apparent.

rescue center

Animal shelters are fast becoming the most obvious places to find a new pet. This is wonderful, as so many cats are in need of new homes through no fault of their own. Queens coming into a rescue center may give birth while they are there, so kittens are sometimes available.

However, adoption agencies are usually extremely careful where such kittens are homed. You are likely to require a home check and to answer many questions about your experience with animals and your home environment. You will probably be instructed to have the animal neutered as soon as he or she is old enough and may have to sign a document to this effect.

The majority of kittens raised in rescue shelters make wonderful pets. Bear in mind, however, that kittens brought into a center older than seven or eight weeks may have had poor socialization during the critical period. This is especially true of ex-feral kittens or strays who have had little or no contact with people or a domestic home. These kittens are often heart-breaking, as no matter how much time and effort is spent on helping them to gain confidence, there is no guarantee that they will fully recover and become outgoing, friendly cats.

newspaper advertisement

Sometimes, litters of kittens are advertised in local newspapers or

right *Farm kittens may have had little contact with people—beware.*

magazines. These can be genuine attempts by private individuals to find good homes for an unexpected litter of kittens.

However, make sure that you go through the same health and behavioral checks as you would if purchasing a kitten from a breeder. Housing a large number of cats in one place increases the risk of disease, and kittens from such establishments should be avoided if there appears to be more than one litter of kittens available for purchase at the same time.

the internet

Believe it or not, it is now possible to go to a web site on the Internet and purchase a kitten using your credit card! While the Net can be an ideal source of information on finding the right kitten and caring for him or her, this is not the way to purchase an animal of any kind.

Always go to see the environment that your prospective kitten has been raised in and meet the mother. Walk away and look for another litter if anything that you see does not reassure you.

right *Neglected and starving, these kittens were saved by a rescue center.*

choosing a healthy kitten

Sadly, sick or unhealthy kittens rarely survive. Even those that just seem a little quiet or listless for a day can suddenly deteriorate, so choosing a healthy kitten is vital. While some diseases and illnesses can be difficult to diagnose without full veterinary support, the health check outlined below is easy to follow and quick to carry out. Any reputable breeder should be happy for you to pick up and handle kittens if you are serious about buying one.

eyes

A kitten's eyes should be clear and bright. There should be no sign of discharge or watering and no redness. Make sure that the third eyelid is not drawn across the eye, even partially. This membrane comes across the eye from the corner and indicates poor health.

Some years ago, Siamese cats often had squints, and although this eye defect has been largely eradicated, it is still worth checking for.

ears

The inside of the kitten's ears should be pale pink, not inflamed or covered in brown wax. Wax and/or itching may indicate the presence of ear mites, while any odor or discharge are signs of an ear infection. Both conditions require veterinary treatment.

left *Bright, clear eyes, clean ears, and a healthy coat are signs that the kitten has been well raised.*

above *Check the skin's elasticity and the fur for signs of fleas.*

mouth and nose

The mouth should be clean and sweet-smelling. The milk teeth should look clean and healthy.

The kitten's breathing should be regular and easy. Any rasping or wheezing should be regarded with suspicion, as should any discharge from the nose. Cat flu is surprisingly common in young kittens and is often fatal. Unscrupulous breeders may try to pass off these serious symptoms by saying that the kitten has a cold.

coat and skin

The coat should be free from any signs of parasites. Black specks in the coat may be flea dirt—which is usually much easier to spot than the fleas themselves. Fluffing the hair in the wrong direction while holding the kitten over a piece of damp white paper proves whether this is the case, as flea dirt dissolves dark red when damp.

The skin itself should feel loose and movable over the bones and body and should spring back easily into position if gently pulled away at the back of the neck.

limbs and tail

The limbs and tail should be straight, with no kinks or curves. The kitten should be able to walk, run, and jump without any kind of limp and it should hold its tail upright in greeting without unnatural bends or kinks.

anal area

Gently lift the kitten's tail to inspect the anal area. This should look clean, with no redness or soiling present, which may indicate a digestive upset or that the kitten has been licking this area.

overall appearance

Overall, the kitten should look balanced and lively. The stomach should not be distended, as this can indicate a worm load, and the lungs should sound clear and healthy.

All the kittens in the litter should be active and alert. Do not be tempted to take the runt of the litter, or any kitten who is quiet or looks unwell. Even healthy kittens may be at risk of infection if one kitten has already succumbed to illness.

kitten behavior
in the litter

Faced with a whole litter of kittens, it can be hard to tell them apart, let alone choose one to bring home! However, if he or she is going to fit in with your home and family, it is important to choose the kitten with the right personality.

the extrovert kitten

The outgoing kitten may be the one to choose if you are an extrovert yourself! A busy family with lots of noise and commotion will send a more introverted kitten running for cover and may always be too hectic for an anxious animal.

The extrovert kitten is usually easy to spot. He is normally keen to rush toward you. At home, he will want your affection and can be quite demanding. After a short while this kitten will probably need more entertainment, which he may find by pouncing on another kitten, a toy, or by diverting his attention to the drapes.

This is not the kitten to choose if you are elderly, quiet and retiring, or live alone, or if you intend to keep your kitten permanently indoors, as you may find yourself facing a constant battle to keep your cat amused.

the average kitten

The average kitten is usually happy to be picked up, content to play with his littermates, and relatively calm, but still playful. This kitten is ideal for most homes, as he will be able to adapt to busy households, yet amuse himself happily when the household is quiet.

This kitten usually offers the best of both worlds in a good combination of affectionate behavior and independence.

the shy kitten

This kitten may be sitting alone or at the back of the litter. Physically healthy, he prefers not to be in the middle of the mayhem that his

left *A shy kitten is a good choice for a quiet household.*

littermates cause. He will still be happy to be picked up and handled, and indeed, may settle down in your arms or on your lap very quickly and become reluctant to move.

These kittens often grow to be devoted to their owners, sometimes to the point of being clingy, and are often best sharing their affection with another, more confident kitten by being homed as a pair. This prevents the shy cat suffering torment when their owner goes to work and leaves them. A loud, busy household, however, may be too much for the timid kitten.

like father, like son

Some fascinating research indicates that a kitten's personality may be inherited from the father's genetic material. This would mean that the father's sociability has a direct influence on the kitten's future sociability, despite the fact that most kittens never meet him! Of course, the mother's genes affect the kitten's characteristics too, but this influence is compounded by her behavior, since she influences them after they are born.

The full extent of the paternal effect is yet to be fully understood, but it means that your kitten's general personality is already established by the age of around eight weeks. While it is possible to increase sociability through learning over the following weeks and months, it is impossible to dramatically change how outgoing or introverted the animal is overall

left *This confident kitten is sure to become a well-loved companion.*

preparing the kitten's new home

Bringing your new kitten home is exciting, but it may be a little nerve-wracking for your kitten. With this in mind, it is sensible to have made plans about where your kitten will sleep, what he or she will eat, and what your strategy will be for making introductions to the family, other pets, and so on.

room by room

All new kittens feel more secure if they only have to explore one room at a time. This means that they can familiarize themselves with the layout and find their food, water, and litter box, rather than be overwhelmed by the whole home. The kitten is able to start making the room smell more familiar by laying down his or her scent by rubbing on objects and simply walking around in that place.

Choose the kitten's first room before leaving to collect your new pet. Most owners choose the kitchen, simply because it is the easiest room to clean and the family is likely to gather there on a regular basis. A den or even a quiet bedroom is just as good, so long as you can shut the door to restrict your kitten's movements in the first few hours or even days. Many owners are uncertain about restricting their kitten's movements, but cats regard confinement as security, and you will be helping your kitten to find his feet in his new home.

Once you have decided which room your kitten will be introduced to first, check it thoroughly for dangerous

right *To prevent rivalry problems, each kitten or cat needs its own food bowl.*

56

objects. Small items such as elastic bands and paper clips are choking hazards, while electric cables and fragile ornaments are best removed or covered.

As soon as your kitten comes into this new room, he is likely to smell whether or not it is safe and familiar. It is possible to trick your kitten into thinking that he has been there before by rubbing a cloth around the walls and furniture that has recently been in contact with his and his mother's scent glands (see pages 31–32). Cats feel far more secure in places marked with their cheek pheromones.

Once your kitten feels secure in this one room, encourage him to rub onto a new piece of cloth, which can be used to rub the walls and furniture of the next room that you wish to introduce.

A new product called FeliFriend has been introduced in several countries to help cats and kittens feel more secure in new surroundings. FeliFriend is a synthetic substitute for the cat's own facial secretions, and since it is odorless and invisible to humans, it can be used in the same way on walls and furniture. Ask your veterinarian about this product before you bring your kitten home if you wish to give your pet the benefit of modern science!

other basic necessities

Food

Make sure that you have a supply of food that the kitten is used to. Even if you intend to change your kitten's diet later, allow him to settle in for at least a week before very gradually making the change.

Water

Your kitten may be thirsty after his journey and finding the water bowl is an important part of orienting himself to the new environment. Decide in advance where you are going to position the water bowl and leave it there for the first couple of weeks.

above Even a four-week-old kitten will use a litter box if it is carefully chosen and positioned.

Stomach upsets are relatively common in kittens. They are often caused by a combination of stress and a change of food, or even a change of water. It may be worth using still mineral water from a store for your kitten's drinking water, at least for the first few days. Once he has settled in, cold water from a faucet will do fine.

Bed area

There are many different kinds of beds to choose from (see page 67), but the most important factors are that the kitten's bed smells familiar and feels cozy. Placing a cloth or blanket that has come home from the breeder in the bed will help to make it smell reassuringly like home.

Litter box

Make sure this is prepared and ready for your kitten as soon as he comes through the door. You don't want your kitten's first experience in his new home to be an accident on the carpet! Put the box as far from the kitten's food, water, and bed area as the room allows.

traveling with your kitten

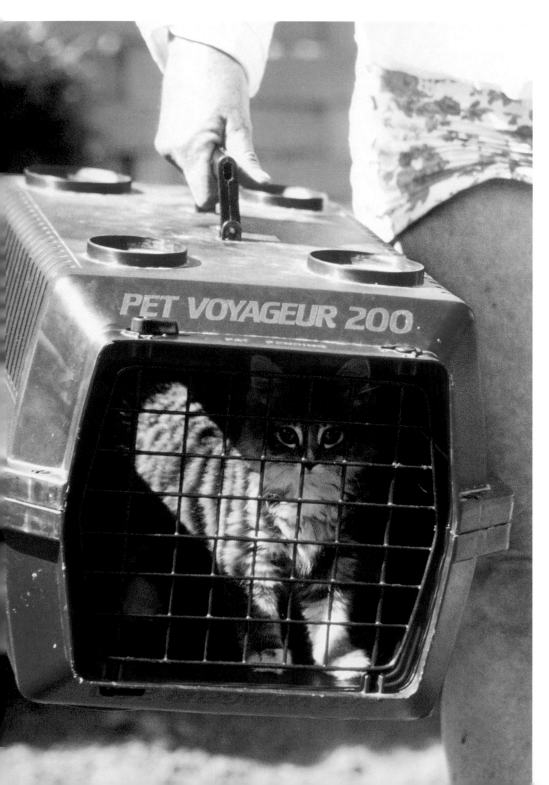

Before you set off to collect your kitten, think about what the forthcoming journey is going to feel like from his point of view. The chances are that this will be the kitten's first time away from his mother and littermates, and the first time he has been in a car. Both these events will seem very strange to your kitten, but with forethought it is possible to make the whole transition easier.

traveling container

It is essential that you obtain some kind of traveling container to transport your kitten home. Kittens can become frightened when faced with new sights, sounds, and smells, and can jump from your arms and run away in fear if they are not safely confined.

Traveling containers come in a variety of shapes and designs. Cardboard carriers are useful as temporary containers. However, they can become weakened by moisture, and as a nervous kitten may urinate in the bottom of the box, this is not ideal. Cardboard boxes are less than ideal from the kitten's perspective, as he will not be able to see out of the box on the journey.

Far better are plastic-covered wire-mesh carriers. These are usually rigidly built, with a carrying handle on the

left *Kittens should always be transported safely, no matter how short the journey.*

top. These allow safe, secure carriage of the kitten, while retaining good visibility. Old towels and newspaper can be put into the bottom to make a cozy nest. These carriers are also ideal when introducing your kitten to other pets at home (see page 61–63), especially as he will feel secure in it by the time you reach your destination.

the smell of security

Whatever basket or carrier you bring your kitten home in, you need to make sure he feels comfortable inside it. One useful trick is to place something familiar from the kitten's nest inside the box before you intend to use it. This can be an old towel or a piece of cloth that the kittens and their mother have been lying on at the breeder's home. Placing this in the carrier at least half an hour before the kitten allows the familiar scent to spread a little. When you put the kitten inside, he will think that he has somehow been there before!

Kittens often find the motion of an automobile upsetting on the first journey. Some cry or meow continuously. Try to ignore this as much as possible, but reassure and talk to your kitten all the time while he or she is quiet. It is sensible not to feed the kitten before traveling, as this may cause car sickness. If the kitten vomits, wait until you are home before cleaning up, or else your kitten may have a chance to escape.

seasoned travelers

Some well-traveled cats become so used to the car or other vehicles that it is simply a home away from home. This is simply achieved by familiarity:

above *Mesh sides give security and allow visibility.*

if you wish your cat to be a good traveler, you need to regularly take your kitten out for short journeys until he becomes used to it.

avoiding the carrier

The reason many cats disappear when they see a carrier or traveling container is that they associate it with going to the veterinarian. Leaving the carrier or basket out around the house makes it become "part of the furniture" to your cat and it will begin to smell familiar. Your pet will be less reluctant to go inside it on other occasions.

introducing your kitten to the home

Having brought your kitten home, placed him in his special room, and shut the door, what next? The chances are, he will be eager to explore! Try to keep everything calm and quiet. Keep children at bay for the first few minutes, while you try to focus the kitten's attention on the litter box. Once this has been used, his adventures can begin.

safety first

Be aware that most kittens immediately want to hide or explore behind objects. This means that closing cupboard doors, blocking access to the back of the oven, and closing the washing machine door are all sensible precautions.

children

If your new kitten has met children before, their sounds and movements probably won't be a surprise. However, if your kitten has not yet encountered children, or he feels a little overwhelmed, make sure that you supervise carefully and take each step of the introduction gradually.

Children should be encouraged to sit on the floor and remain as calm and quiet as possible. Teaching even very young children to wait until the kitten comes to them is an excellent practice,

left *Babies and young children should always be supervised when meeting kittens and cats.*

as the worst possible scenario is a frightened kitten being chased by an over-eager child. First impressions matter, and it is important that child and kitten form positive associations from the outset.

Once the kitten has approached the child, gentle petting can begin. You should discourage children from picking up the kitten, as this is where accidents can occur and kittens can become panic-stricken. Children are always eager to make friends with the new pet, but they need to understand that the kitten needs frequent rest periods and he should not be disturbed when he is asleep.

introducing a resident dog

Dogs and cats can be best buddies if given the opportunity! If you are unsure how your dog will react to a kitten, be safe and keep him on a leash and the kitten in a pen or crate to begin with.

Most dogs chase cats because they are excited by the movement, rather than wishing to cause harm. Keeping the kitten secure and unable to run is therefore the best policy in the early stages of introduction. Using a large dog-sized cage or kittening pen for the kitten to live in for the first few days or even weeks allows dog and cat to sum each other up and cope with new smells, sights, and sounds with the protection of bars between them.

After this, controlled introductions with close supervision are required. During first meetings where the kitten is out of the pen, the dog should be kept on the leash and the cat should have several high vantage points to escape to. Seek help early if you feel that your dog represents a threat to your kitten—it is always better to be safe than sorry.

left *Introductions to dogs and other animals should be carefully controlled. These kittens are clearly apprehensive.*

introducing
your kitten to a cat

One of the most common causes of behavioral problems in cats is a poor introduction to another cat in the household. This first meeting can make or break the relationship forever, and even if you are sure that your adult cat will love the new kitten on sight, it is worth taking every precaution to ensure that things go well.

Faced with an intruder in the center of their den, most cats choose to flee rather than fight. However, if the established cat feels threatened or cornered, he or she may well choose an aggressive option. There can be nothing more distressing for a kitten facing an older, unfamiliar cat than to be subjected to a vicious attack and be chased behind the couch, or even out of the cat door. This is a perfectly understandable response from your older cat's point of view, yet it will leave him or her traumatized, too.

Like us, cats need time and space to make new friends. There is no reason why an adult cat should love the stranger in the home any more than you would love a burglar! To make friends with a person, we observe social rules— smiling, shaking hands, and getting to know each other. Cats are no different. They need to become familiar with the other pet's smell, sight, and sounds before they become friends.

left *First impressions count! Keep the introduction between kitten and resident cat controlled.*

controlled introductions

1. Bring your kitten home and familiarize him with one room only, shut away from your other cat. Do not allow them to meet for the first day or two. During this time, frequently stroke the kitten, then immediately feed your adult cat and stroke him. This begins the "scent exchange" process.

2. With your adult cat secured in a room or out of the house, take your kitten into another room and allow him to explore for a short period of time. Return the kitten to his familiar room, then bring your adult cat into the room where the kitten has just been and allow him to sniff. Reassure him and feed him to increase his sense of security. Repeat this with the other rooms in the house.

3. Put your kitten into a kittening pen or wire-mesh traveling crate. Feed him there and make sure he is comfortable and relaxed. Place the kitten in the pen or crate on a raised surface, if possible, and feed him some delicious food.

4. Bring your older cat into the same room and immediately feed him delicious food, such as cooked fish or chicken, on the floor, well away from the pen. This is the first time that the cats have seen each other, and although their smell will be familiar to each other, you may need to intervene if the older cat shows any sign of aggression. Make a loud noise or use a water pistol to interrupt any hissing, spitting, or flying at the bars. Do not use your hands to intervene, as you may be injured.

5. If both cats are calm, reassure them and allow your adult cat to investigate. How your adult responds will depend on his personality and how much work you have done to integrate their scents. Finish the session calmly by removing the kitten from the room and taking him back to his room.

below *This kitten's defensive posture reveals its anxiety. Use a wire basket to ease introductions.*

6. In between these sessions, continue to play with your kitten alone in other rooms of the house. This continues to establish his presence as a permanent fixture through scent.

7. Don't rush the cats' first face-to-face meeting. Sometimes it's helpful to place the existing cat in the pen while the newcomer is free to wander in the same room. Watch the cats' body language carefully. When they are content to feed side by side, the next step is to feed them at the same time, without the pen as a barrier.

8. How long this process takes depends entirely on the individuals concerned. Some take just a few days, while others take weeks. Once the two cats will feed calmly together, the chances are they will accept each other as friends. Rubbing each other, washing each other, or sleeping curled up together is a sure sign that things are going well.

when things go wrong

Occasionally, despite all the right introductions, an adult cat and a kitten refuse to get along. This may be a personality clash—after all, we don't get along with every person we meet! If your kitten and established cat are feuding, despite your best efforts, ask your veterinarian to refer you to a feline behavior specialist for extra help and advice.

kittens and babies: fact and fiction

No other animal/human combination seems to cause more controversy and worry than cats and babies. Urban myths have developed around the hygiene

right *Young children and cats should always be supervised.*

aspects of keeping cats and children together, as well as the basic practicalities. Even some doctors and health visitors seem unsure of the realities of any such

risks and may add to a parent's confusion, rather than alleviating it.

As with so many aspects of life, keeping pets and children together simply requires a healthy dose of common sense. Domestic cats offer no more potential risk to human health than any other animal, and provided that basic household hygiene is observed, this risk can be eliminated completely.

toxoplasmosis

Perhaps the greatest fear for any pregnant woman is of infection and subsequent risks to her unborn child. Expectant mothers are sensibly warned about the risks of toxoplasmosis during pregnancy.

Toxoplasma gondii is a protozoan parasite that can be passed to humans. Cats can carry the parasite, having eaten infected wildlife, and pass it via their feces (see page 133). This makes it sensible for pregnant women to wear gloves when gardening, and when emptying or cleaning litter boxes—or even better, get someone else to do it!

However, cats are not the sole source of toxoplasmosis: it can be transmitted through eating undercooked meat, or vegetables grown in contaminated soil.

If you are worried about the risks from toxoplasmosis, or are planning to have a child and already keep cats,

it may be sensible to ask your GP to do a blood test to show whether you are immune to the infection.

Immune mothers cannot pass the infection to their unborn child. A lack of immunity simply means that you have not been infected previously, thus making sensible hygiene precautions a priority. Keeping your kitten off work surfaces where food or bottles are to be prepared and frequent hand-washing are basic necessities for any family.

Once a baby is born, parents are often worried that their cat or kitten may present a risk by climbing into the crib and suffocating the baby by lying on it. This is highly unlikely! It is only in the early weeks that babies are unable to turn over or move themselves, and although most cats and kittens like to find warm and cozy places to sleep, they do not usually appreciate the noise, smell, and disruption that goes with a baby in a crib! Basic precautions during this time, such as putting a cat net over the crib and ensuring that baby and kitten are not left unsupervised, offer peace of mind.

Kittens usually readily accept babies as new members of the household. However, kittens and babies need a great deal of time invested in them in their early weeks and months and this is a tall order for a new mother, particularly if the kitten is not able to go outside the home. Indoor cats are forced to rely on their owners for all their mental and physical activity, as well as needing a litter box indoors, which can add to the work and time investment.

Think carefully about getting a new pet at the same time as having children. There will always be an opportunity to add to the family later—perhaps when the children are old enough to help care for your pets.

left *Basic hygiene prevents any health risks in pregnancy.*

basic equipment

Cats do not require vast or expensive arrays of accessories. However, a few items will help to settle your kitten into his or her new home. The rest are essential only if you are a doting owner or a compulsive shopper!

essentials

Food bowls

Dishes should be sturdy and non-slip. China, plastic, and stainless steel bowls are all suitable. Saucers are not ideal, however, as kittens tend to tip them over and paddle in them, with obvious results! One dish for food and another for water is a minimum requirement and these should be kept and washed separately from the family's plates and cutlery.

Litter box

Many different designs of box are available. The most basic are open boxes, while others are hooded, and some even have cat flaps in the front, which offer security, particularly if

left *Most cats enjoy the security of a high-sided bed that they can snuggle into.*

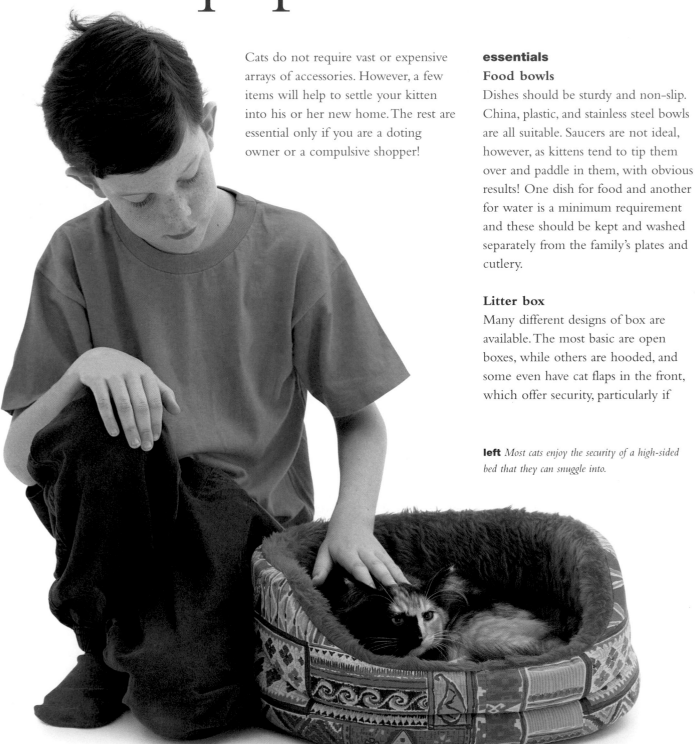

other pets in the household are likely to ambush the kitten while he or she is trying to use the toilet!

Most kittens prefer a loose, fine grade litter in the box, rather than clumps or pellets.

Bed

All kittens need a place to sleep that they can call their own. While your favorite armchair may soon become your pet's sleeping place, at least at the outset your kitten should have its own bed. The bed could be a cardboard box, plastic basket, a fabric "snug," or a duvet. Fake fur or "sheepskin" materials placed in the bottom of a bed will make it warm and inviting to most kittens. Hammock style beds can be hooked neatly over radiators, offering extra warmth.

Whatever you choose, your kitten's bed should be easily cleaned and washable, as bedding can be a ripe breeding ground for fleas.

Crate/pen

Although it may look like a cage, an indoor kennel, crate, or pen is an ideal way to save your sanity during the first weeks your new kitten is at home. Kittens can get into all sorts of trouble when they are not supervised—they can chew electric cables, fall out of windows, and escape from the house all too easily. Crates or pens also make introductions to older cats, dogs, and other animals far easier and less traumatic for all concerned (see page 62).

Collar

If you are going to use a collar for your cat's identification and safety, make sure your kitten gets accustomed to wearing it early on. Make sure it is a safety collar that will break or stretch under tension.

Identification can be an engraved disc, a small barrel, or a plastic label holder. Make sure it is not too heavy for your kitten to carry around.

right Scratching posts need to be tall enough to accommodate the adult cat at full stretch.

Scratching post

Prevention is always better than cure, and a scratching post could save your best furniture! All cats need to scratch to shed the outer layer of their claws, keeping them in good condition. Many cats also scratch trees and posts to mark their territory (see page 108).

A scratching post can be a log from the yard or a post with sisal wound around it. It should be tall enough for an adult cat to stretch up to, and stable enough that it doesn't topple when in use. Carpet-covered posts are best avoided as this may sanction your kitten to scratch carpet in other areas of your home.

Brush or comb

No matter what kind of coat your kitten has, it is essential that he or she becomes used to being groomed from an early age. This not only promotes a healthy skin and coat, it also assists in building your relationship with your pet. Friendly cats groom each other to maintain social bonds—and we can do the same. A soft brush, velvet mitt, or comb also allows your kitten to become used to being touched with an object, and to make pleasant associations with it. This makes examination and inspection at the vet less frightening.

nutritional care

your cat's needs

All cats are obligate carnivores. They are designed to be expert hunters, so they are not able to eat a vegetarian diet—a cat fed solely on a meat-free diet without very specific protein supplements will die. This is because cats need specific nutrients found only in animal tissue, such as vitamin A and niacin, and are unable to manufacture an essential amino acid called taurine, which is vital for a cat's eye function.

how much to feed

Like people, different cats need different amounts of food. Cats utilize protein for repair of body tissue, growth, and energy, and kittens particularly need to be given frequent opportunities to boost their energy levels.

If you are feeding a complete, dry food, you will probably find that your cat will return to his food on many occasions during the day and night to snack and will regulate himself as to how much he needs to eat. Canned and moist foods cannot

below *Your kitten's diet needs will depend on its lifestyle.*

be fed in this "ad lib" manner, so a kitten of eight to 12 weeks will probably need five small meals a day to allow his digestive system to function properly.

where to feed
On the whole, cats prefer to feed where they feel secure. This usually means that they feel more comfortable feeding on a raised surface, rather than from the floor. The position that you

choose to feed your kitten should be quiet and well away from the litter box. It should also be protected from the advances of other cats, and dogs, who find it almost impossible to resist the smell of moist cat food.

what to feed
It is essential that all kittens are fed on a diet that reflects their energy and growth requirements. A huge amount of research has been done by pet food companies to

above *Dried foods assist dental hygiene.*

ensure that kittens are catered for in the optimum way, and these diets ensure that your pet is given everything it needs for healthy growth and digestion.

Some owners prefer to offer a non-commercial diet. However, this is a complex process and it can be very easy to omit vital requirements at this sensitive time in your cat's development.

If you wish to change your kitten's diet, always do so very gradually. Changing what you feed your pet too rapidly can cause serious stomach upsets and diarrhea. Always consult your veterinarian if you are unsure about any aspect of feeding or nutrition.

drinking water
Fresh, clean drinking water should always be available for your kitten. Although cats fed on a moist food are likely to gain most, if not all their water requirements through their food, those fed on dry diets need to drink more

below *Place your kitten's feeding dish in a quiet location. There are many to choose from.*

frequently. If your kitten suddenly starts drinking more water than normal it may be unwell, so consult your veterinarian if you are worried.

Milk should not be given to kittens or adult cats. Contrary to popular belief, cow's milk is not tolerated well by many cats and can cause diarrhea. Once weaned, kittens do not need milk in their diet. However, cat milk is now available in many supermarkets, and small amounts of this specially formulated product can be given as a treat, if you desire.

types of food

Pet food is now big business! In one store alone, it is possible to choose from over 30 kinds of cat food, ranging from tins of meaty chunks to dry kibble. Your choice will probably depend on the age of your kitten, what he or she is already used to eating, and the convenience and cost of the food.

Moist food

This term describes cat foods that are packaged in a can or vacuum-sealed pack. Typically, they contain a lot of water—anything up to 80 percent. These diets are usually manufactured to look like meat, either compressed into the can or formed into chunks.

above *Kittens need to learn how to eat solid foods during weaning.*

right *Cats can be fussy eaters. Try to find a healthy diet and stick to it.*

However, the look and smell of the food does not necessarily reflect what is in it.

High quality, easily digested protein is essential for kittens and adult cats, and this can only be determined by looking at the list of ingredients. Unfortunately, these can be rather vague, as descriptions such as "meat and animal derivatives" do not describe which kind of meat source is used.

Moist foods are usually highly palatable. Indeed, in recent years, obesity in cats is more frequently seen by veterinarians and this may be attributable to the sedentary lifestyle of our cats and their food!

Dry food

Dry foods are usually formed into small nuggets by an extrusion process. Again, it is important to investigate the ingredients of the food. Dry foods have the advantage that they can be left out indefinitely for "ad lib" feeding, allowing cats and older kittens to regulate their feeding across the day.

"Low calorie" and even "dental health" versions of dry foods are available. These are worth considering, as periodontal disease is very common in cats and can result in the loss of teeth, as well as infections of the mouth and gums. Crunchy dried foods may contribute to your cat's dental hygiene, as chewing it helps to clean the teeth.

Treats

Many cat owners like to reward their pet or give it a treat by offering tidbits. The many commercial brands of food treat can be well utilized in training and can strengthen the bond between you and your kitten.

However, it is highly inadvisable to allow your kitten to steal food from your plate or to feed human foods that could present a risk to your animal's health. Cooked chicken bones, for example, are highly dangerous, since they can splinter and puncture the digestive tract.

Stomach upsets in kittens are commonly caused by feeding inappropriate foods. One poor kitten had to make repeated visits to the veterinarian after being encouraged to try a curry meal by his well-meaning owner.

exercise and play

Just like us, cats need a combination of good food and exercise to stay in tip-top physical and mental health. Most felines manage this themselves, by regulating their nutritional intake and running, jumping, and hunting outdoors at will. Indeed, cats are designed to use energy in short bursts. The rest of the time they are quite happy to conserve their resources by sleeping in front of a heater!

However, in recent years the increased palatability of cat foods and an increase in indoor living has meant that obesity in cats is far more prevalent than it used to be. Making sure your cat has some sort of exercise is therefore important, and this can easily be done by playing with your kitten and encouraging him or her to interact with toys.

toys

The range of cat toys on the market is huge and varied, from small catnip mice to room-height activity centers ideal for indoor cats (see page 94). They can be divided into a few basic types:

Interactive toys

These puzzle-feeders intermittently reward the kitten with food when playing with the toy, or are designed to stimulate the kitten's interest in moving objects. Some of the best of these have a small ball trapped inside a circular track, which moves alluringly as the kitten tries to catch it.

left *Some cats find the smell of catnip toys almost irresistable.*

Catnip toys

These are often furry mice, sisal balls on ropes, or other small shapes that can be picked up and carried like prey. Some cats respond to the smell of catnip as if it gives them an enjoyable "high;" it is thought that the scent of catnip or cat mint affects areas of the brain that induce a feeling of euphoria. This harmless effect is only seen in a small percentage of cats—the rest may play with the toy but do not seem to enjoy the same exhilarating effect!

Wands/rods

Wand toys are ideal for people who want to play with their kittens. Consisting simply of a length of rod with a long piece of string attached to its end, feathers or other toys can be tied to the end of the string and waved around, while the kitten chases this "quarry." Such toys are excellent for teaching kittens to chase and pounce, while keeping human hands and feet well out of the equation.

Clockwork and battery-operated toys

Clockwork mice, spiders, and even frogs are available for your kitten's entertainment. These offer real fun and activity, as long as they are well supervised. Kittens may be tempted to pounce on such toys and chew them, so it is essential to check that any plastic or fabric attachments are held securely in place.

New versions of these old favorites, such as battery driven balls that roll and twist at random when switched on, are lots of fun for large, confident kittens, but beware of frightening a more nervous cat on the first few occasions it encounters a particularly active or noisy toy.

Homemade toys

Some of the most effective and best-loved toys for cats are cheap and simple. Kittens love paper bags—a bag blown up with a puff of air can keep them amused for hours! For some variety, place a small lightweight ball in the bag or put the bag into a safe cardboard box so that the kitten has to climb in and out to play with it.

left *Cat activity centers offer hours of fun, plus they offer vantage points and built-in scratching posts.*

Lengths of string and large rolled up balls of foil attract most kittens, and even the quietest cat will come out of its shell to pounce on one of these. However, safety should always be a priority, so never allow your kitten to play unsupervised with such objects.

below *Cats love movement! If your pet is reluctant to play, try waving a toy on a piece of string or elastic cord.*

games to play with your kitten
Food scattering

If you are feeding a dried complete food, there is no reason why your kitten should not do a little "hunting" for it. Rather than feeding it from a dish, why not throw the food into the yard, or even around the den, and allow your kitten to search for the scattered pieces. This uses the kitten's sense of smell and natural abilities to hunt to their full advantage, as well as making mealtimes more interesting.

Teaching your kitten to retrieve

How easy it is to teach your kitten to retrieve will depend on his motivation to play and to learn, his confidence, and to some extent, even his breed. Orientals and Burmese cats often seem to retrieve naturally, while others may take a little longer!

However, carrying prey is natural behavior, and many cats can become adept at chasing, picking up, and carrying toys, and then bringing them back to their owner to be thrown again. This provides an ideal opportunity for stimulation and exercise, particularly for indoor cats, as many hunting games need to be simulated if they are to remain content.

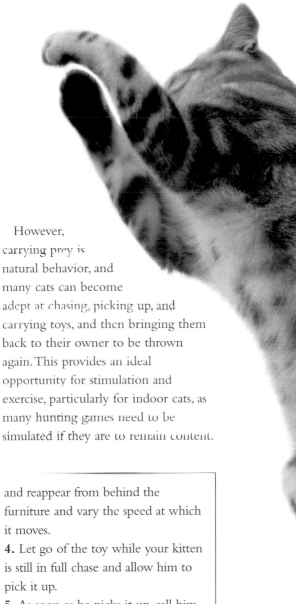

How to teach your kitten to retrieve

1. Be patient! Your kitten will need to learn this new skill in his own time. Do not become frustrated or disappointed if he doesn't understand immediately.

2. Teach your kitten to come to you when called (see page 100).

3. Find a toy that your kitten likes and is happy to play with. Have a really good game with it, dragging it along the floor and allowing your kitten to chase and hold it. The more "prey-like" the toy is and the more it behaves like a small rodent, the more your kitten is likely to show an interest, so make the toy disappear and reappear from behind the furniture and vary the speed at which it moves.

4. Let go of the toy while your kitten is still in full chase and allow him to pick it up.

5. As soon as he picks it up, call him to you and offer another toy or a piece of food as a direct swap for the item. Do not have a tug of war with your cat for the toy. If he runs off with it, entice him back and have another game, rather than attempting to take the item away.

6. Be persistent and practice. Many cats learn to run out after a small toy or piece of rolled rag and carry it back to their owner, just like a dog!

attention and correct handling

One of the main reasons why most owners keep cats is the physical contact and affection that they show. However, not all kittens automatically enjoy being touched and handled by people. This is partly determined by genetics, partly by the kitten's experiences before the age of seven weeks, and partly how his or her new owner handles him.

picking up your kitten

Kittens only enjoy being picked up if they feel secure. Place one hand under your kitten's chest, with your fingers spread between the front legs. Scoop him up and support his bottom with your other hand. If you are going to carry your kitten, bring him in close to your chest so that he feels safe.

Children should never pick up a kitten without adult supervision, as a kitten who does not feel secure may try to jump down, injuring itself or the child in the process.

approaching and stroking

It is very bad manners to approach a cat and offer it attention! Cats always like to be the ones who initiate attention and feel much more comfortable when they are allowed to do so. An anxious kitten's worst nightmare would probably involve

left *Kittens feel secure if handled gently yet firmly.*

being pursued around the house by an eager owner, only to find itself trapped under a bed, with the owner peering down at it in a vain attempt to make friends!

Allow your kitten to come to you, particularly if he is a little nervous and has hidden somewhere initially. As soon as he starts to move toward you, turn your body away slightly and narrow your eyes. (See talking to your cat, pages 34–35.)

Once physical contact has been initiated by your kitten, stroke him around the ears and face to begin with. If this is happily accepted, move on to stroking down your kitten's back and up his tail.

Move your hand slowly and carefully and try to stay relatively quiet. Anxious kittens often flee to the other side of the room if their owner sneezes or moves suddenly while stroking.

Few cats enjoy being touched on their bellies or their feet. Although some cats learn to roll over and be petted, this takes time and a trusting relationship with the owner. It is far better to start with areas that your kitten clearly enjoys and build your relationship from there.

hand care

Your hands should always mean safety and pleasure to your kitten. Smacking your cat, or playing rough games where your kitten chases your hand and pounces on you, are both totally

inappropriate ways of interacting with a cat. Many owners of adolescent or adult cats rue the day when they taught their pet to play predatory games with their hands as "prey." This type of behavior may be amusing when the cat is young, but can be worrying and even dangerous when it becomes an adult.

abolish slavery!

Although it is important to allow your kitten to initiate interactions between you, this needs to be tempered against becoming a slave to your pet's desires! Some bold cats are so good at demanding attention that they wake their owner in the middle of the night—by meowing or using their paws or even their teeth—in

order to be fed, get attention, or just for fun!

Make sure that you are the one to decide when your kitten gets attention by initiating play on occasions when you have time, and rewarding calm, sensible behaviors when your kitten solicits attention. He or she needs to know that you enjoy interacting, but that you do not always leap to your feet to pet or feed him or her every time you are asked.

below *Keep your hands at a distance when playing with your kitten—it's safer for both of you!*

grooming

right *Grooming should start young. Kittens need to become accustomed to rigorous physical maintainance.*

All cat owners know that cats are scrupulously clean creatures and that they groom themselves impeccably. However, kittens need to become used to being handled all over and some cats, such as longhaired varieties, need regular brushing and combing to prevent matting and skin problems.

Like all types of training, the earlier that you accustom your kitten to being groomed, the easier it will be. In the case of long-coated breeds, it is essential that mats are not allowed to form, or the kitten's first grooming is likely to be an unpleasant experience that will make it afraid of brushing and combing.

equipment

Brushes: The type of brush you need depends on your kitten's coat. A soft bristle brush is usually adequate.

Comb: A metal-tooth comb is ideal for removing dead hair. Make sure that the teeth have rounded ends that will not scratch the skin.

Velvet glove: Ideal for putting a shine on smooth-coated cats. Most kittens really enjoy being stroked with this type of mitt.

Cotton balls: These are useful for wiping ears and eyes. Ensure that you use a clean piece for each job.

Nail clippers: Guillotine-action clippers are usually the safest choice.

right The grooming tools required will depend upon the type and length of your kitten's coat.

brushing

Brushing should be an enjoyable experience for your kitten. Hold him gently on your lap or a table, and start by brushing gently along your kitten's back. Move on to brushing his legs, head, belly, and tail. Be gentle and watch your kitten's responses carefully. Stop if you think that he is becoming agitated or fearful.

combing

Comb through the hair in the direction that it grows. Be cautious not to tug or pull. If you find a matted clump, it is better to remove it completely with scissors rather than risk hurting your kitten with the comb.

using a glove or mitt

Putting a really healthy shine on your kitten's coat couldn't be easier with a soft glove or mitt. Simply stroke your kitten in the direction of the coat to polish each hair.

cleaning ears

Cleaning your cat's ears should rarely be necessary. Indeed, when a kitten's ears look or smell dirty, it is likely that he has an infection that needs treatment from the veterinarian, rather than simple cleaning. Never poke any object or cotton balls into the ear. The inside of the ear flap can be wiped gently with baby oil, or dampened cotton ball.

cleaning eyes

Some cats suffer from tear-staining under their eyes, particularly the flat-faced breeds. Tear stains can be difficult to remove, as they are so close to the eyes. A dampened cotton ball may do the trick, or ask at your local dog and cat grooming center for a special no-tears stain remover.

cleaning teeth

Tooth decay and gum disease are real problems among many domestic cats. This is primarily due to diet, but can be influenced by good dental hygiene.

Cats should have their teeth cleaned at least once a week—preferably every day—but for most owners this is unrealistic. If you intend to clean your kitten's teeth and be an example to cat owners the world over, make sure you start when your kitten is very young, so that he can more easily become accustomed to the experience. Special cat toothpastes are available, best used on a finger brush, so you can carefully control the brushing around teeth and gums.

Remember that kittens lose their deciduous or milk teeth by the age of around five months. Check in your kitten's mouth every week. Mouth ulcers and sore gums can easily go unnoticed unless you become familiar with the normal state of your pet's mouth.

bathing

Generally, cats rarely need bathing. However, it may be necessary to remove unpleasant substances from the coat occasionally, to give a skin treatment, or to prepare a cat for a show.

If you are going to bathe your kitten, have all the necessary equipment ready on hand before you begin. Apart from specific breeds, such as the Turkish Van, most kittens loathe being immersed in water, and hate being lathered with shampoo even more!

Bathing is best done in a wash basin, using warm water and a special feline shampoo. You will need to hold your kitten firmly with one hand, while using the other to tip water over his coat. Make sure that all shampoo is thoroughly rinsed out, and dry your kitten with a towel by wrapping it around him gently and cocooning him inside.

Very few kittens or cats will tolerate the sound and feeling of a hairdryer near them, so it is best to remove as much moisture as possible with the towel and then keep your kitten warm until he is thoroughly dry.

clipping nails

For the vast majority of cats and kittens that lead an active, indoor and outdoor existence, nail clipping is unnecessary. However, a small percentage of individuals—particularly those that live only indoors—nail clipping is needed. Clipped nails can also help when a kitten scratches furniture, or people, inappropriately.

If you intend to clip your kitten's nails yourself, start by accustoming him to the sight and smell of the clippers. Your kitten also needs to get used to remaining still while you hold his foot and gently extend the claws, so that the tips are clearly visible.

Only clip off the very smallest amount of nail from the tip. It is always possible to remove more later, but causing injury or pain will put your kitten off being handled for a long time.

right *Clipping claws requires patience and practice.*

below *Use a soft brush to gently accustom your kitten to grooming.*

hygiene and litter boxes

Cats are well known for their cleanliness. They spend many hours grooming and preening and are particularly fussy about where they go to the toilet. Indeed, they can be so fussy that even a small level of dissatisfaction can alter their toileting habits—and this can create extensive house training problems.

types of box

There are several types of litter box, the simplest just an open plastic pan. More complex versions come with lids, sides, and a cat flap at the front for access, while others are equipped with a self-cleaning base that filters soiled litter from unused substrate.

types of litter

Studies have shown that most cats prefer loose, rakeable substrates in the litter box. These are soft to stand on, clump forming, and are easy to scrape and move to cover the urine and feces in the box. Fuller's earth and other clay-type litters are popular, too. Wood shavings can be too lightweight for some cats and

left *Many kittens and cats prefer the security of a covered litter box.*

add to the general mess, as they can become scattered around the box.

Some litters are now produced containing scented particles or deodorizing substances. These offend most cats since they smell too strong to feline noses—and can irritate the pads of the feet when damp.

how many boxes?

How many litter boxes you provide depends upon how many cats you have and whether you allow your kitten to go outside to the toilet. Once fully vaccinated and allowed outside, most kittens definitely prefer to go there, as they wish to keep their den area as clean as possible.

As a rule of thumb, there should be one litter box per cat in the household, plus one. This may seem like a lot, particularly if you have several cats, but providing so many toilet areas reduces competition and the potential for stress-related behavioral problems.

where to position the box

It is absolutely vital that all litter boxes are placed in quiet areas, well away from the hustle and bustle of life, and out of the reach of curious dogs and children. Dogs find cat feces almost irresistible and some like to ambush the kitten on the box!

It is also essential that the box is positioned well away from the kitten's eating area and sleeping places. No one wants to sleep or eat in the toilet—indeed, kittens will often choose to go to the toilet outside the box if they perceive that it is too close to their food.

how often should the box be cleaned?

This varies according to the individual cat, but on the whole, most like the box to be scrupulously clean at all times. Some cats would rather use the carpet than a box that has not been freshly cleaned, and some will refuse to use it at all if another cat has been into it recently.

Very occasionally, kittens need to be taught what the litter box is for. If this is the case, placing a small amount of previously soiled newspaper or fabric in the box can help to form suitable scent associations. Bear in mind that your kitten may need to go to the toilet at any time of day or night. This means that the great outdoors, or a litter box, always needs to be accessible.

human health and hygiene

Provided that your kitten is kept in the best of health and is regularly de-wormed, there is very little risk to human health in even the closest contact. However, pregnant women are strongly advised to avoid emptying litter boxes, or should wear rubber gloves when doing so, to avoid the slight risk of toxoplasmosis (see pages 64 and 132).

Kittens and cats of all ages love to use sand as a litter substrate, so children's sandboxes should be kept covered if they are not to be used as giant litter boxes.

identification

Unlike dogs, cats are not legally required to wear identification that links them with their owners. However, in the event of your kitten being injured or lost outside your home, identification is his or her only chance of help and being reunited with you. There are three main forms of identification, and each has advantages and disadvantages.

collar and identification tag

This is by far the easiest and most visible method of identification for your kitten. The major advantage of putting a collar and tag on your kitten is that it is immediately apparent that he or she is owned by someone. This prevents the all-too-common scenario of a kitten being found in the street as a stray and being taken home by a well-meaning cat lover, never to be returned to its rightful owner! Wearing a collar also indicates that the cat is well-cared for, and can even carry a message indicating that it should be taken to a veterinarian in the event of an accident and bills will be paid by the owner.

right *Fitting an ID tag to a safe type of collar is a sensible precaution.*

above *Tattoos, as seen in this cat's right ear, are a permanent form of identification.*

Each year many cats are injured or even killed by becoming entangled in their collars. The most common injury is jaw or leg damage, when the cat has managed to get one front leg or foot through the collar and becomes stuck in this position. Other injuries that can occur involve the cat jumping from a height when the collar is already snagged on a fence post of branch of a tree. In this situation it is possible that the cat can be hanged as it dangles helplessly from the collar.

The best compromise to his dilemma is to use a collar that stretches or breaks under tension. Some of the new "breakaway" collars are excellent and automatically open if tension is placed upon them. Stretch collars usually have a piece of elastic in them that allows the cat to remove its head in the event of it becoming caught up. Both solutions mean that new collars have to be bought when the cat arrives home without one, but this is a small price to pay for safety.

Some collars are also made of light-reflecting material, a safety bonus when your cat is out in the hours of darkness. A reflective collar makes your pet easy to see in automobile and motorcycle headlights.

identichip

Identichipping involves the insertion of a tiny microchip, about the size of a grain of rice, under the cat's skin. This carries a serial number that can be read by a scanner and entered into the chip company's computer to trace the owner's details. The identichip is injected using a hollow needle, usually between the shoulder blades. Most kittens and cats do not find the process too uncomfortable, but is better to wait until very small kittens are larger before inserting a chip.

Microchipping is a relatively reliable method of permanent identification, but depends upon the finder taking the stray cat to be scanned. There is no visible evidence of ownership, and the finder may not think of microchip identification.

tattooing

Tattooing is a common method of cat identification in some countries. It involves injecting tiny amounts of ink under the skin to make a permanent mark in the form of a unique number. In cats this is usually done inside the ear flaps, and may require a general anesthetic.

a **safe** environment, **indoors**

plants

Cats do not seek out edible vegetation in the same way that the canine scavenger may do. However, kittens are notoriously inquisitive, and playful or bored kittens are much more likely to try nibbling on a house plant than those who have their minds fully occupied with other activities. Tender-leaved plants are most tempting in these circumstances, and some, such as Diffenbachia and Cyclamen, are particularly toxic if ingested.

Some plants can cause skin irritation, particularly if the kitten has rolled in the leaves or in the sap from a plant stem that has been cut or damaged. Always consult your veterinarian if you are concerned about your kitten's health, and take along a sample of the plant that the kitten has come into contact with.

below *Some house plants are potentially lethal if ingested by your kitten; this Azalea is safe.*

windows and balconies

Most cats are extremely careful and precise about where and how they balance. Indeed, even a 12-week-old kitten has a fully formed righting reflex that usually ensures that they land safely from a fall, on all four feet rather than other body parts.

I lowever, sometimes things go wrong, and kittens have been known to fall great heights from balconies or upstairs windows, usually with very serious consequences. Keeping upstairs windows closed or using netting may be the only way to ensure your kitten's safety.

foreign objects

Thankfully, it is relatively rare for cats to ingest dangerous articles or substances, but certain items are more common causes for veterinary intervention than others. Sewing thread is an almost irresistible plaything—and if ingested can become wound around the intestines. Cassette tape too can necessitate surgical removal if swallowed, while elastic bands may cause intestinal blockages.

Occasionally, cats and kittens ingest poisonous substances by grooming them from their coats. Indoors, the worst culprits are chewing gum and pine needles from Christmas trees!

Chemical substances are infrequently swallowed, but again may be licked from paws or coat if the kitten walks through them. Tar, paint, and household cleaning substances are the most likely risks.

hiding places

Most kittens love to hide in small, dark spaces in the home. Such places include washing machines, spin dryers, and even fridges. Risks to their health may present themselves in cupboards, where a kitten can settle down to sleep among household chemicals, or where they find the opportunity to play with and chew plastic packaging that contains medicines. Even common medicines such as aspirin are highly toxic to cats and need to be kept safely out of their way. Child-locks on cupboard doors and extra caution when using electrical items are sensible safety precautions when you have a kitten in the house.

a **safe** environment, **outdoors**

If you decide to allow your kitten access to the outside world, the major hazards that he or she is likely to face are manmade, rather than from the natural world. Far more cats are killed or injured on the street than by ingestion of poisonous plants or falls from trees, although occasionally, these do happen. Keeping your kitten indoors at night, but allowing him or her freedom during the day, is a sensible strategy, as cats are easier to see on the street by day and are most likely to cross unfamiliar territory while hunting at dawn and dusk.

outdoor plants

Although many outdoor plants are toxic if ingested, the chances of them poisoning your kitten are slim. Once outside, kittens are usually far too distracted to even think about chewing plants or trees. Combined with their fastidious ways, this means they are usually safe from such risks.

chemicals

Chemicals that have been spilled or left in accessible places may not be so easy to resist. The interiors of outhouses and garages are irresistible to most kittens. Not only do they run the risk of being shut into such places, but they are likely to come into contact with chemicals

left *Ponds should be securely covered with mesh or netting to eliminate the risk of drowning.*

such as car anti-freeze, rat and mouse poisons, and slug pellets, and these may seem like fun playthings at first.

other animals

Cats are flight animals—faced with a threat, they would much rather flee than fight, and this means that they can usually outrun neighborhood dogs. However, kittens are small and vulnerable and can become confused if they are chased by a dog, making

their safe return home more difficult. Other cats probably pose more of a threat, as cat fights frequently lead to injuries such as torn ears, cuts, and subsequent abscesses.

In some countries, venomous snakes and other indigenous wildlife may be a problem. It is always worth chatting to your veterinarian to check on specific local risks and to ensure that anti-venom is kept in supply. Kittens are occasionally stung by wasps and bees, usually after trying to play with them. This painful experience is not normally harmful—but teaches the kitten a lesson!

Frogs and toads may also appear to be tempting toys for a young kitten. In the case of frogs, the kitten is likely to do the amphibian more harm than the other way around, but toads possess mild toxins in their skin coating that is highly distasteful to all other animals. A kitten who attempts to bite or pick up a toad is likely to get a nasty surprise, followed by voluminous salivation and foaming at the mouth. Although long-term harm is unlikely in this scenario, call your veterinarian if you suspect that your kitten has tasted a toad and is having trouble breathing or appears distressed.

going outside

letting your kitten outside

All kittens need to have completed their vaccinations before they are allowed out into the big wide world. Even if your kitten has completed his vaccinations when you bring him home, it is sensible to allow him three or four weeks to become fully acclimatized to your home. This ensures that on the first occasions when you let him out, he will quickly be able to orient himself to his new surroundings and be bonded enough with his new home and family to want to return.

The first time that you let your new cat outside can be quite nerve-wracking. Cats are infamously good at escaping—and even if you have good fencing around your yard, you can expect him to find his way out pretty quickly. How safe this is depends on the area in which you live and how independent your kitten is.

effective fencing

Cats are excellent climbers. Even an eight-foot fence is easily scaled and cannot guarantee that your cat will stay in your yard. Fencing that is angled inward at the top is much more effective, although again, some cats have even been known to conquer this.

If you live in an area that could be considered dangerous for cats—close to a busy street, for example—walking your cat on a harness and leash, or building an outdoor pen, with a mesh roof to completely enclose part of your yard, are the only options for guaranteed safety.

letting your kitten out for the first time

Plan to let your kitten out early in the day. This gives him time to explore and still come home before it is dark. Make sure that your kitten goes out hungry. Cooking some food that has a strong odor, such as fish, before letting him out will encourage him to return rapidly for a meal.

Open the door and crouch down outside, to give your kitten confidence when he first steps outside. Allow your kitten to walk outside, rather than

left *Sights, sounds, and smells of the outside world captivate the senses.*

right *Exploring the garden is part of the kitten's development.*

above *Confident pets quickly learn to come and go as they please.*

carrying him. Kittens have scent glands between the pads of their feet, so as they walk outside they leave a trail of scent that they can follow to find their way home.

Walk with your kitten around the yard or garden, talking to him. After a few minutes, encourage your kitten to follow you back into the house and then feed him.

Over a period of days, repeating this exercise will increase your kitten's confidence. If your kitten has already learned to come to you when called

(page 100), he will be willing to come back inside for a food treat or meal. Try not to be too anxious if your pet explores beyond his usual boundaries.

Although there are risks to your kitten's safety outside, they need to be sensibly balanced with your pet's emotional and physical needs. Cats need to run, jump, hunt, sit in the sun,

1. Your kitten needs to understand that the cat flap is an entrance and exit. Prop the flap completely open, using a lump of clay or a pencil wedged in the hinge. This will allow your kitten to look right though the hole.

2. Start the training with your kitten on the outside, so that he will be moving toward the inside of the house, which represents security. Ask someone to hold your kitten gently outside the door, while you encourage the kitten to come through the hole by luring with a food treat and calling its name. Give the kitten the food treat the instant it comes through the flap. Repeat this several times.

3. Once the kitten has mastered coming in through the hole, you can squat on the outside of the door while he is inside the house and call him through.

4. When your kitten is completely confident with walking in and out through the hole, it is time to gradually lower the flap. This time, the flap should be propped open halfway. Encourage your kitten to push against the barrier to reach you and his reward on the other side.

5. Once the kitten is confident in pushing the flap a tiny amount, from both sides of the door, lower the flap another inch and let your kitten practice at this level. Most kittens soon adapt to this new experience and learn to push the flap the whole way.

and behave just like cats—and being outdoors is a great part of the quality of many cats' lives.

learning to use a cat flap

Installing a cat flap for your kitten has advantages and disadvantages. Having learned how to open the flap, your kitten will be able to come and go as he pleases, and this reduces the need for a litter box in the home, as most cats prefer to toilet outside. However, for some cats, learning to use the flap can be a terrifying experience, so always take time to help your kitten to learn.

As with all training, work one stage at a time, and only continue at your kitten's pace. Never try to push your kitten through the flap, or push its paws or head against the door to attempt to show it what to do. There is a risk that you could make your kitten afraid of cat flaps with this physical ordeal.

no exit

If you intend to keep your cat in at night or at any other time, it is a good idea to signal to the cat when he is not able to use the flap as an exit. Although we can see that the flap is locked in place, a cat may not understand why it cannot push the flap open when only minutes before a single shove with the front paws worked beautifully!

Placing a "signal" next to or across the flap is a useful strategy, as the cat learns to associate the signal with the cat flap being shut and gives up any attempts to break out. The signal can be anything convenient—a towel hung up next to the flap could read "no exit" to your kitten, as would a piece of board placed across the flap. This system works very well as long as you put the signal out every time that the flap is shut and remove it when the flap is open again.

keeping an indoor cat happy

If you have decided that the risks of allowing your kitten outside are too great, or behavior problems prevent it, it is essential that you offer lots of mental and physical stimulation indoors instead. Sadly, a large proportion of cats with behavioral problems are those who are kept indoors and lead a boring and understimulating life. This is particularly relevant to those cats who are alone during the day. Without company, the hours between breakfast and dinner must seem very long indeed, and it is vital that such cats have something to occupy their minds.

fun with a friend

Life is undoubtedly more fun with a friend! If you intend to keep your kitten indoors from the outset and you know that he will spend considerable amounts of time alone while you are out at work, it is sensible to consider getting two kittens from the same litter. Opposite sexes usually socialize best, but neutered brothers and neutered sisters can also be best buddies.

If this is not possible, think about how much time you are going to be able to devote to your kitten's entertainment when you get in from work. Quality time with your kitten will be even more important.

left *Indoor cats need mental stimulation as well as affection if they are not to become over-dependent.*

food toys

Several types of commercial toys encourage your cat to play. Puzzle feeders in the shape of a ball or cube are filled with the kitten's dry food, and he or she needs to learn how to roll the toy along to get the food out. In a more natural state, cats need to work for their food through hunting and stalking, and these toys simulate such activity.

novelty toys

Most kittens love playing with pieces of string, balls, and feathers tied to the end of a wand. However, if you are not there to make the toy interesting, how much will your kitten play?

Novelty is the secret here. In order to keep your indoor cat active and stimulated, a new object or toy needs to be introduced every day. This hones your kitten's ability to explore and be adventurous.

Providing novel toys need not be complicated or expensive. A safe, open-topped cardboard box can be an adventure playground one day, turned over with a door cut in the side it can be a place to play hide and seek on another occasion. Hiding a ball underneath provides stimulation in a

different way, and putting the ball inside the righted box will create hours of fun while the kitten chases it around the box walls.

Once your kitten has played with the item for a day, put it away somewhere, and present it again a week or two later in a different way. Your kitten may remember the toy, but it will never become so familiar that it is boring.

activity centers

When planning activities for your indoor kitten, try to think in three dimensions. Outdoors, your kitten

above *A variety of toys, bought and homemade, keep cats amused and non-destructive.*

would stalk, chase, run, and pounce. However, he would also climb—and would spend time and energy balancing on the tops of fences, in tree branches, and on walls.

Special cat activity centers can be purchased to simulate this experience for your cat in your own front room. These can be as tall as a room, with shelves and resting ledges jutting out. Some models screw tightly to the wall, so that your kitten can jump onto, climb up, and leap from it without fear of the structure falling. Activity centers can be expensive, but homemade versions are often just as good.

left *The play's more fun with two!*

home videos

If all else fails and you find that your kitten is home alone and bored, there are even video cassettes for your pet to watch! Specially designed with images that cats love, the videos have soundtracks designed to attract feline attention, too. Goldfish swim in and out of the screen and moths appear to be caught inside the television. The perfect gift for the kitten that has everything!

choosing a cattery

Going away and leaving your kitten in someone else's care may seem a worrying prospect, but finding a good cattery will put your fears at rest and allow your pet to become used to this kind of accommodation early in life. Catteries with a good reputation always get booked up very quickly, especially for summer vacations and the holidays, so finding your pet a cattery and booking it far in advance is essential.

how to find a cattery
Recommendation is by far the best way to find a good vacation home for your kitten. However, it is still important that you visit the cattery to check the accommodation and see

for yourself how your pet will be housed. Good catteries are always happy for you to have a look around, although they should not allow you to have contact with the animals in their care.

Catteries should always accommodate cats from different homes separately, to avoid any risk of cross-infection and to ensure that disputes between strange cats do not occur.

what to pack

The first and most important item to remember to pack for your kitten's stay

left *Kittens usually adapt well to a short stay in a cattery, especially if friendly faces pay a visit.*

in a cattery is his vaccination certificate. All catteries should check this carefully and refuse to house any cat that is not fully vaccinated against contagious diseases.

Any medication that your kitten needs should be taken, and the cattery staff should be made aware of dosage rates. An extra charge may be levied for administering medicines or giving special foods, so ask before you book your kitten for his vacation.

Some catteries are happy for you to take an item of your clothing or a towel with your household's scent on it, to reassure your kitten during his stay. Toys are welcomed by most catteries, as long as they are safe to leave with an unsupervised pet.

above *If you own more than one cat, it may be preferable to house them in the same cattery.*

alternatives

For people who can't bear to leave their pet in a cattery, home-sitting services are a reliable alternative. Home-sitters not only feed and care for cats, they also keep your home and yard in a clean and tidy state in your absence!

However, for cats who are very dependent on their owners, it can be more distressing to be left at home with a stranger than going to a cattery. This is because cats regard the interior of their home as their security—having it invaded by a stranger can make them anxious and insecure.

behavior

how kittens learn

All intelligent living creatures are subject to the laws of learning. While most dog owners recognize the need to train their puppy, few cat owners realize that their pet can be trained and

right *Tail up! This is a classic greeting gesture.*

that their cat is training them instead. Kittens learn about the world through discovering which behaviors bring rewards and which don't. Just like us, they are more likely to repeat a behavior that gets rewarded—whether

or not this behavior is one their owner appreciates or not!

Kittens view rewards in different ways than we do. For example, most owners tend to think that rewards for their kitten include stroking, petting, treats, and being fed. However, to your kitten, exploration, freedom, stolen food, play, attention, and even eye contact can be rewarding, too!

For example, your kitten is in a playful mood. He climbs your drapes just for fun, and discovers a thread hanging from the top. This makes a great toy, and he spends several minutes pulling and scratching at the fabric. Finding this behavior highly rewarding, he is sure to climb your drapes again in the future.

But that's not all. On entering the room, you discover your kitten's antics

and remove him from the drapes, talking to him all the while to show your displeasure. However, rather than thinking that you are annoyed with him, your kitten thoroughly enjoys the attention and knows how to get your attention the next time he's feeling bored!

Much problem behavior in adult cats is learned in this way. Cats adore attention—some learn to cry in front of their owners to get what they want, others even use their claws or teeth to gain their owner's eye contact, physical contact, and vocal contact.

Other unacceptable or inappropriate behaviors also become established through accidental rewards—a kitten that climbs onto a work surface and finds his owner's Sunday lunch, for

example, is likely to repeat the behavior in the future. Equally, a kitten that urinates in an inappropriate place may find that the relief it feels afterward potently reinforcing—and may repeat the behavior.

All in all, one simple rule helps to remove all confusion about how cats learn: reward all the behaviors that you like, and try to ignore or interrupt any behaviors that you don't. Kittens learn incredibly quickly using this process; your pet's future behavior will be determined by it.

discipline and punishment

Cats of all ages respond very negatively to punishment. Felines are flight animals—they would much rather flee at the first signs of threat than deal

above *Bright-eyed and alert, this kitten is inquisitve and ready to learn about the world.*

with it head-on. Punishment simply breaks down the relationship between cat and owner and reduces the trust between them.

Smacking, shouting, tapping on the nose, and grabbing by the scruff of the neck are all punishments that should be avoided rigorously—they will only compound your kitten's inappropriate behavior in the long-term and may even create further problems through the anxiety and stress they can cause. If your kitten has a behavior problem, see pages 102–119 or consult your veterinarian, who will be able to refer you to a feline behavior specialist.

training your kitten

All training with your kitten needs to be done in small stages, and at your pet's own pace. Be patient. If your kitten does not seem to respond in the way you would like, think about what the animal's perspective of the experience may be. You may discover that he or she was learning something quite different than what you intended!

coming to you when called

This is a most useful exercise, which can also add to your kitten's general safety. Being able to call your cat in from the yard ensures that he can be located at any time, and means you can spend "quality time" with your pet when you decide.

1. The way to a cat's heart is through its stomach! Each and every time you are going to feed your kitten, call him to you first.
2. To begin with, call your kitten from only a few feet away, then feed immediately with a food your kitten really enjoys.
3. Gradually extend the distance that your cat will come when called and give praise, affection, a treat, or dinner.
4. Never call your cat to you and then do something unpleasant. This includes spraying with flea spray, nail clipping, and bathing. Your kitten will quickly associate the negative experience with coming when called and choose to stay away.

sitting on cue

Why teach your kitten to sit on cue? Well, why not?! Cats are just as easily trained to perform basic exercises as dogs, as long as the methods used are reward-based and enjoyable.

left *Treats have to be given to reward correct behavior and reinforce training.*

1. Use a delicious piece of food to gain your kitten's attention.

2. Lift the food over and above his head so that he has to look right up at you.

3. As he lifts his head, his bottom will lower and then hit the floor. Say "good" as soon as this happens and give the treat. If your kitten jumps up to get to your hand, ignore him completely until he is standing again, then lure some more.

4. Practice in many different situations until your kitten is reliably placing his bottom on the floor when you lift your hand. Now you can add the cue word "sit" just before he sits to get the food.

walking on a harness and leash

If for some reason you have decided that it is too perilous to allow your kitten out of doors alone, training him to walk on a harness and leash can offer a safe compromise. Although some owners train their cat on a harness so effectively that they can exercise him outside their yard, it is probably more realistic to use this method to give your cat some freedom within the confines of your property.

Cats can easily become fearful of the environment and the restraint presented by the harness, if they are unused to them. Be patient in the early stages and allow your kitten to become accustomed to wearing the harness in his own time.

1. Put your kitten in the harness for a few seconds, without the leash attached, while you play with or feed him.

2. Gradually extend the period that the kitten can wear the harness in the home. The kitten should be completely relaxed while wearing it, which may take some time to achieve.

3. Attach a short, very lightweight length of cord to the harness, so that you and the kitten get used to the feel of having something attached to the harness.

4. Holding the end of the string very gently, allow your kitten to wander at will for a few seconds, preferably lured by a food treat that you are holding in the other hand. If your kitten starts to move away, drop the cord or follow the kitten.

5. Never jerk or pull on the cord to restrain the kitten, nor allow the kitten to play with the end of the cord.

6. When your kitten is happy to walk on the harness and cord, swap the cord for a light leash. Practice in short, fun sessions, walking around the home.

7. When your kitten is totally relaxed about wearing the harness and leash, you can venture out into the yard. Again, take the training slowly and allow your kitten time to explore and become familiar with the new sights and sounds.

below *Lifting a tidbit of food above your cat's head automatically eases it into a sitting position.*

behavioral problems

By far the most common behavioral problems reported in kittens and cats are messy problems! These usually separate into two categories: house training problems and marking problems. Both types can be caused by a clinical problem. This makes it essential that any kitten or cat who is urinating or defecating inappropriately indoors is taken to a veterinarian to rule out any medical cause.

house training problems

Cats are normally fastidious creatures and want to make every effort to ensure that the interior of their home or den stays clean, too. This makes an "accident" somewhere in the house even more distressing, both for the owner and the cat!

There are several potential causes for house-training problems. The solutions may be simple. If, having tried the suggestions below, the situation still

left The type of litter and position of the box can affect your kitten's house training.

has not improved, ask your veterinarian for a referral to a behavior specialist without delay.

Possible cause: Some kittens simply never learn to be clean. This may be because they have not had the opportunity to practice toileting in a litter box and covering the deposits properly with litter afterward. Kittens born into deprived environments may try to toilet somewhere safe and quiet, because early associations with litter were never properly formed.

Solution: Never punish a kitten for toileting in the wrong place. Use a biological detergent and odor-absorbing crystals from your veterinarian in the area he chose to use. If he has chosen a corner to toilet

in, put the litter box there and fill it with loose, fine-grained, rakeable litter.

Placing a small amount of previously soiled material into the box can help to build early associations there. Some kittens feel more secure if the box is covered with a lid. Praise and reward your kitten for even stepping onto the litter box.

Possible cause: The kitten is not happy with the type of litter box, its position, or the litter material within it.

Solution: Thoroughly clean the areas that the kitten has inappropriately soiled using a biological detergent and odor-absorbing crystals. Make sure that the litter box is well away from the kitten's bed and food areas. No one likes to eat near a toilet.

Try changing the type of box. Some kittens like a top, some like a top and sides, while large cats and kittens simply need a larger box!

Try changing the type of litter. The fine-grained, loose substances tend to be preferred, but some kittens can be extremely fussy and will only use fine soil, peat-based products, or even sand.

Possible cause: Bad associations with the litter box. Some litters contain deodorizers that can make the kitten's footpads sore. The kitten may have a stomach upset and feel discomfort while on the box. The most common bad associations are caused by owners who ambush the kitten while on the box to give it a pill, and dogs or other cats that approach the kitten while it is compromised.

Solution: Make sure the litter used is favored by the kitten. Reposition the box away from dogs and provide several boxes if you have several cats. Never ambush the kitten while it is on the litter box.

marking behaviors

Cats communicate through smell and can utilize the smell created by urine and feces to signal how they feel. The most common feline response to stress or anxiety is to use the smell of urine for reassurance. Unfortunately this is highly unpleasant for humans, especially as kittens often choose to urinate or defecate in a place with a high concentration of their owner's scent. The owner's bedclothes and shoes are favorite places for kittens to leave a deposit.

By far the most important factor in eliminating these sorts of messy problems is to eliminate the kitten's anxiety or stress, as this is the cause. Sometimes simply moving to a new home can trigger stress and its subsequent response. In these cases time is often the cure, so long as the behavior is not allowed to become habit-forming.

All kittens need security and need to build relationships with everyone in the household. Barring the kitten from unsupervised areas where he might be tempted to urinate or defecate is therefore sensible in the meantime.

below *The familiar scent of its sprayed urine reassures a nervous cat.*

spraying urine

Urine spraying is the cat's number one choice to relieve stress—and sometimes to protest, too! A few cats even learn to perform this behavior to get attention from their owners—and it certainly works! If your kitten is spraying urine in the home, seek medical and behavioral advice if the "first aid" treatment below is ineffective.

Possible cause: Fear of "invasion" of their territory by another cat or an unknown threat. This is relatively common among kittens who use a cat flap to go in and out of the home. The kitten realizes that other cats exist beyond the four walls of his precious domain, and that they may invade his core territory.

Solution: Close and block the cat flap to test the theory! Thoroughly clean the areas where the kitten has inappropriately soiled using a biological detergent and odor-absorbing crystals obtained from your veterinarian. Feed your kitten at the previously soiled areas and make sure you give him lots of love and security. Never punish a kitten or cat for soiling in the home—it will only increase anxiety and make matters worse.

Possible cause: A new object (or human!) arriving in the kitten's home. Typically, nervous or under-socialized cats are more likely to react to new furniture or visitors to the home who do not smell of the "clan odor" that gives them security in the den. Some kittens mark the new object or person with urine or even feces to make themselves feel more secure.

Solution: Clean the areas where the kitten has soiled using a biological detergent and odor-absorbing crystals. Try to encourage your kitten to rub his facial glands on a piece of

above Sprayed urine marks territorial boundaries; cats may reinforce them if their home is "invaded."

clean cloth in the same way that he would rub you in greeting. Do not try to force your kitten to do this—wait for him to make the first move. Rub this cloth along the edges of the new furniture to make sure that it smells of the "clan odor" to the kitten. Ask your visitor to rub the cloth on their hands and shoes. Sometimes taking shoes off outside the home can help.

Possible cause: Conflict with another cat in the home.

Solution: This is a complicated scenario that affects any existing cat(s), as well as the kitten and his owner. The "threat" cannot be removed, since your older pet is at least as important as your new kitten. Seek professional help without delay.

crazy half-hours

Kittens are well known for suddenly having a "crazy half-hour." Owners will typically report that the kitten suddenly jumps up, adopts a strange expression, and then performs a "wall-of-death" act around the den! The kitten usually makes unusual side-stepping movements and curves his spine. His tail often forms into a strange inverted "U" shape and his ears are held back.

Possible cause: Such behavior is often linked with time and the kitten's feeding regime. If the behavior occurs regularly an hour or two after feeding, it may be that the choice of diet is not suiting the kitten particularly well, and that a free-feeding regime on a complete dried cat food may be better.

In essence, crazy behavior is not harmful. It is simply a way for the kitten to release some pent-up energy that would normally be used during the evening for hunting, if he was living a wild existence. Sometimes this behavior stops automatically as soon as the kitten can go outside and have more exercise.

Solution: For some kittens, the learning experience they can have during crazy half-hours can lead to behavioral problems. This is usually because their owners make exciting noises during their mad activity, and this can lead to the kitten becoming more predatory in its actions.

Kittens may learn that flying around the room at top speed causes everyone to stop what they are doing, look at them, and laugh. Even worse, they may discover that biting or scratching humans as they run past brings even more excitement, screams, and squealing. Unfortunately, such behavior can quickly become established and bright kittens may discover that they can manipulate their owners' attention and movements by biting them and running away.

right *Poetry in motion! This kitten is all fired up, as the fluffed tail indicates.*

left *Focusing your pet on appropriate play helps to release energy and calm hyperactive behavior.*

calming inappropriate play

Kittens need to release pent-up energy, in the same way that children often do. A good game with a feather or toy attached to a long wand or piece of string helps to engage the kitten's interest without attracting him to your hands or feet.

If you find that your kitten repeatedly targets your hands and feet for unwanted attention, use "active ignoring" to remove his fun. This means putting on an Oscar-winning performance of disgust by immediately standing up, walking out of the room and shutting the door. The kitten will be left alone, slightly bemused. If you respond like this consistently over a period of days, your kitten will learn that only gentle, friendly interactions gain your attention.

Although it may be difficult, once you have eliminated your kitten's diet as the cause, ignoring crazy behavior is the only way to ensure that it does not become a problem in the future. Leaving the room, or even wearing gloves and boots so that the kitten cannot gain a reaction from biting, may be the solution.

These kittens normally need extra stimulation in their lives. Plenty of play with appropriate toys—never hands or feet—is required.

scratching and over-grooming

Apart from indoor urination, scratched furniture has to be the most common problem cats can cause in the home! All cats scratch, but whether this is acceptable or not depends on where and what the cat is scratching. If the scratching is performed on trees or posts in the yard, the owners may be unaware that their cat does this at all. Equally, if the scratching is on a post supplied for the purpose indoors, all is well. If, however, the item of choice happens to be a new piece of furniture, scratching is a problem!

Cause: Scratching is a necessary action for cats. Contrary to popular belief, they do not do it to sharpen their claws, but to remove the outer husk from the sheath of the claw, which reveals the new outer coating underneath. Cats also have scent glands between their pads, so that scent is released onto an object when a cat scratches it, leaving a mark for other cats to "read" by smell, along with the visual marker.

Solution: First, ask yourself whether your cat has the opportunity to scratch naturally. If your cat is kept permanently indoors, or does not go out very much, an indoor post is essential. This should be tall enough so your cat does not reach over the top

left *Scratching is normal cat behavior; it removes the claws' husk and releases scent.*

above Healthy kittens groom themselves thoroughly, but some over-groom to reduce stress.

when he stretches his front feet upward from a standing position. Bear in mind that however small your kitten, he will soon grow, so buy a post that will be tall enough for him as an adult. The post needs to be covered with sisal or other scratchable material. Praise your kitten every time he uses the post to scratch.

To prevent your kitten scratching the wrong surfaces, try to ensure that he cheek-rubs them instead. Research has shown that when cats are feeling secure, they mark objects and people using the glands in their cheeks. Where they do this, they rarely scratch or spray. Encourage your kitten to rub on your hands or a clean cloth, then rub this over the furniture. Feeding your kitten on these areas can also help.

If this problem persists, look at where your kitten is scratching. If it is near a door or window, it may indicate that he is anxious about another cat coming into the home. If so, try to remove the cause of the stress by blocking the cat flap or even access to the window.

over-grooming and self-mutilation

All cats groom themselves, but if this is done to excess, the result can be a loss of coat from the affected area, and even damage to the skin in extreme circumstances.

Possible cause: Sadly, some cats and kittens become so anxious or overwrought about real or imagined threats to their security that they can damage themselves. They groom and even nibble themselves obsessively as a

way to reassure themselves, causing harm, over a period of time. In other cases, there is a simple physical cause, such as fleas or a skin problem.

Solution: Such behavior is very rare in kittens but occasionally occurs. If you suspect that your kitten is over-grooming, make an appointment with your veterinarian as soon as possible. Many of these cases have a clinical cause, and medical treatment for flea allergy or dermatitis needs to begin quickly. If no medical foundation is discovered, referral to a behavioral specialist may be needed.

pica, chewing and dribbling

Kittens are notoriously curious. Just like human toddlers, they are into everything and test the world by putting things into their mouth. This habit is even more tempting if they work out that they can get extra attention by biting or chewing objects that they are not meant to have, and long-term and dangerous behavioral problems can result.

pica and chewing

Pica is the term given to the ingestion of inappropriate or unusual items. Kittens seem particularly attracted to plants and may chew on house plants and swallow them if not prevented from doing so. While it is perfectly normal for cats to chew and eat small amounts of grass, some house plants are poisonous (see page 86).

Possible cause: Some kittens learn to chew plants for attention, while others may be indicating that they lack fiber in their diet.

Solution: Changing your kitten's diet or offering cat grass to eat may solve the problem. Cat grass can be bought from pet stores as a kit and grown on a windowsill.

Possible cause: Unfortunately, pica seems particularly common in some Oriental breeds. This behavior can start with chewing on fibrous items, such as cotton fabric and wool, and can result in all manner of items being chewed and sometimes swallowed. Electric cables may be on the list of these cats' delicacies, with fatal results.

Solution: Consult a behavior specialist if you think that your cat may be persisting with this behavior after obvious diet changes and prevention. Some Orientals are so obsessed with this behavior that the provision of small, safe quantities of fabrics may have to be offered. There is evidence that this could be a genetic anomaly, so it is always best to seek professional help and check that the breeder's stock does not perform this behavior before you buy from him or her.

left *Playing with wool and cord is normal, but eating it is cause for concern.*

above *Pica—the chewing of items not intended for consumption—seems more common in Orientals.*

dribbling and kneading

When they are cuddled and content, some kittens regress to the time when they were with their mother and dribble in anticipation of a milk feed. Some may even knead you with their front paws in order to stimulate milk production! While some owners find this behavior endearing and enjoy the closeness it brings, for others the thought of their kitten dribbling over them spoils the growing attachment with their new pet.

Cause: Once your kitten is established in your home, he will start to regard you as his family. In your cat's eyes, you take on the role of mother, providing food, security, warmth, and resting places. Some kittens take this to heart and can actually behave as they would with a real feline mother.

Solution: If your kitten takes his role as your "baby" a little too far, simply reduce the intensity of your affectionate interactions with him and play with him more, as an alternative way to enjoy contact.

predatory **behavior**

One of the great fascinations of living with cats is that they are wild animals that have chosen to live as domestic creatures. As predators, many cats like nothing more than catching a small animal and bringing their kill home to you, their owner. This behavior harks back to the instincts that cats have to provide food for their families. As your cat's "family," he is honoring you with the proceeds of his hunt!

Many owners find their pet's predatory behavior repulsive, for a number of reasons. Not only do cats love to chase and hunt small creatures that appear to be totally defenseless to us, but cats also seem to want to torture them before killing them. Nearly all kittens and cats "play" with their victims and some even walk off disinterested as soon as the "plaything" becomes still, even if it is not dead. Well-fed cats may not attempt to eat their prey—especially as some of their quarry, such as rat, is reported to taste unpleasant.

Cause: Although thousands of generations has altered the cat to some extent, the wild side of our

left *Owners often have to learn to accept their cat's predatory behavior.*

for this reason that kittens and cats chase, bite, and kill small rodents, birds, and insects.

Solution: Extra feeding is unlikely to stop a cat from wanting to hunt. Indeed, some studies have found that cats would leave a dish of delicious cat food to chase and kill a rat, then return to the dish to continue feeding!

Some owners at least give birds and rodents a warning that their cat is hunting by attaching a bell to the pet's collar. In most cases this is unsuccessful—the cat learns to move very carefully to avoid triggering the sound of the bell, or leaves his strike to the very last second, when the warning comes too late to save the victim.

For the vast majority of owners, accepting that their cat hunts is all part of ownership. Indeed, for many households in certain cultures or environments, this is the very reason why cats are kept—they do an excellent job of reducing the rodent population in farms and stores. However, in urban areas, cats are sometimes responsible for decimating the local bird population, and this is

above *Designed for survival. The cat's athleticism and predatory instinct is demonstrated.*

when pressure can be placed on cat owners to prevent their pets from doing what comes naturally.

Most cats' favorite times to hunt are at dawn and dusk. This is the time when the cat's prey is most abundant. Keeping your kitten in during these times may be the only answer, and certainly reduces the number of catches, if not stopping the behavior altogether.

aggression

Although aggression toward humans is rare, when it does occur it is nearly always a serious matter. Nearly all cases where kittens or cats show aggression should be seen by a veterinarian to rule out medical problems as the cause, and then referred to a behavior specialist if the veterinarian cannot help.

Aggression from cats may seem trivial when compared to the same problem in dogs, for example, but this is not always the case. Cat bites can be particularly dangerous—not because of the injury itself, but because of the risk of infection that can result. Cats carry many different types of bacteria

right *Inappropriate, predatory play in youth can result in aggressive behavior when the cat is an adult.*

in their mouth, and a cat bite drives these bacteria deep into a narrow wound, making it impossible for the infection to escape. All cases of cat bites should be seen by a doctor and treated with antibiotics.

petting and biting

"Petting and biting" accurately describes kittens and cats that seem to enjoy being stroked and petted, then suddenly become wild-eyed and lash out at their owner's hands, with their claws or teeth. Such cats usually flee their owner's lap immediately after and settle a short distance away to wash—as if in embarrassment.

Possible cause: This behavior seems to be a result of the combination of domestic and wild that is in every cat. On the one hand they clearly enjoy close contact and being petted, while on the other they may suddenly feel trapped and need to escape.

Solution: The ideal treatment for this problem requires patience. The kitten should be petted for only 10–20 seconds at a time while being watched carefully. If the kitten goes still, its ears go back, or its eyes widen, the petting should stop immediately and the kitten encouraged to get off the person's lap. Ideally, all interactions should end on a successful note, to encourage the kitten to come back for more petting next time. All punishments are counteractive—even shouting can make matters worse.

predatory or play "aggression"

In essence, predation involves no aggression! We are not angry with our food when we eat it, and cats are not aggressive when they pounce on prey. However, where cats learn to redirect predatory behavior onto humans in their household, this is the best term we have. Some cats that perform predatory

above *Hunting instincts can spill over into the home, where hands and feet become prey.*

behaviors toward their owners go to great lengths to "ambush" them as they come home from work, walk up the stairs, or lie in bed.

Possible cause: The majority of these cases have a history of the cat playing with their owner in an inappropriate way. Sometimes, members of the family have played with the kitten using their hands or feet as "prey," which may be funny when the kitten is tiny, but is not nearly so pleasurable when an adult cat pounces on your foot as it hangs out of bed!

Solution: Increased play using toys that are clearly distanced from hands and feet usually works well. Cat "wands" are excellent for this.

aggression toward other cats

Unlike dogs, cats are not truly a social species. Although many co-exist with other cats quite peacefully, this is more to do with the resources available—beds, food, and space—than it is social bonding. Some cats who are brought up together, whether littermates or kittens from different mothers, become very attached to each other, and this is obvious from the way that they behave. However, neither of these reasons means that any cat *should* get on well with any other—and they often don't!

aggression to another cat in the home

The causes of aggression to another cat in the home are varied. The most common is where an introduction between a kitten and an older cat has been unsuccessful (see page 62). However, even relationships between friendly cats can break down, and when it happens they can be very difficult to restore.

Possible cause: One cat fails to recognize its "friend" after the other has been to the veterinarian's. These cases are always rather sad. The cat may not recognize the returning pet primarily because he has picked up scents from the vet's and now smells very different. Cats recognize each other by scent, not sight, so a familiar cat can seem a complete stranger.

Solution: Prevention is much better than cure. Before reintroducing one cat to another, rub your hands over the cat who has been left at home, and then stroke the other one before bringing him back in. This will create a "scent exchange" so that the returning cat still smells familiar. Alternatively, take both pets to the veterinarian at the same time!

Possible cause: Redirected aggression can occur when one cat is peering out of the window and becomes aroused at the sight of a strange cat invading the yard. The tension mounts in the watching cat, and this can be triggered if he is interrupted by another cat in the household simply walking past.

Solution: These cases are infamously difficult to resolve. Contact your veterinarian for a referral to a behavioral specialist.

aggression toward cats outside
Possible cause: Aggression to strange cats outside is almost impossible to

above *Defense of resources can be the cause of aggression between pets.*

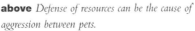

left *If cats are temporarily separated, unfamiliar scent can make the returning cat seem like a stranger.*

cure. Cats are independent creatures and once out of our view, really are a law unto themselves. Some cats can be terrible bullies—walking into other cats' homes and eating their food, spraying urine, and even fighting with them in their own territory.

Solution: If you come into contact with the local despot, take steps to ensure that your kitten's territory and den are well protected. Discourage other cats from approaching the house and fit a magnetic cat flap, or close it up completely if you think there is a risk of invasion.

Occasionally bullies can be so disruptive in a neighborhood that a time-share agreement between neighbors has to be reached. This allows the bully to have freedom at a designated time, and be restricted at other times to allow other local cats to go out safely.

fearfulness

Excellent rearing and good early experiences should protect your kitten from being too fearful when he first arrives in your home. A little insecurity is to be expected with all kittens at first, but continuous hiding or fleeing at the smallest sound means that your kitten needs extra help, care, and attention to fit in with the family.

Possible cause: A kitten that came from a socially deprived background, or is ex-feral, may experience problems in your home. The only creatures he will be familiar with are his mother and littermates, so humans and other animals—even other cats—could seem strange and threatening.

Solution: First and foremost it is essential to realize that cats do not like to be approached, particularly if they are nervous. This means that it is vital to be patient and wait for the kitten to come to you for attention, rather than trying to force him to accept affection.

If your kitten runs and hides for the first few days, let him. Contain him in one room so you know where he is and can give him extra security. Make sure there is a clean litter box in the room and a dish of water, as well as a cozy bed area, perhaps tucked under a box or table so that extra security is added.

Several times a day, go into the room with small amounts of delicious food for the kitten, such as fish or cooked chicken. Sit quietly on the floor with the food a little way from you and wait. If your kitten decides to be brave and emerge from his hiding place, do not try to touch him, but talk to him quietly in a soft voice.

After several repetitions of this routine, your kitten should realize that you always arrive with food, and he will start to emerge as you enter the room. Sit on the floor each time and only stroke him gently when he is eating. If at any time your kitten chooses to retreat into his hiding place, allow him to do so.

Some kittens, particularly those that have been feral up until this point, can be so fearful that even allowing humans to see them in daylight can take several weeks of careful and patient planning and waiting. Once the kitten has started

below Extreme fear: the ears are almost parallel to the head, pupils are dilated, and the lips drawn back.

to form bonds with you, it is time to encourage other family members to do the same. As soon as the kitten is becoming confident with other people, he can be introduced to another room, and finally the whole house.

Unfortunately, there is no rushing a kitten when it is fearful, and sadly, despite the best of efforts, some kittens never gain total confidence. In these circumstances, fearful kittens are nearly always best suited to homes that are calm and quiet. Nervous kittens who grow into nervous cats may suffer almost permanent stress in a busy, noisy household, and their immune system may even be weakened by the stress, leaving it more vulnerable to infections and illnesses. If you are concerned about the long-term effects of stress on your kitten, seek early help.

below *Cats choose "flight" over "fight" where possible, and seek a hiding place if an escape route cannot be found.*

choosing a veterinarian

Even if your kitten is perfectly healthy when you bring him or her home, it is essential that you register with a veterinary clinic immediately. All kittens need vaccinations to protect them against potentially fatal diseases, and your clinic will inform you when these need to be administered. It is also sensible for your pet to have a general

health check at this early stage. Minor ear infections and other relatively trivial problems can quickly become more serious if they are not detected early. Perhaps more important, you need to build a relationship with your veterinarian and feel secure knowing that emergency treatment is readily available.

Sadly, there is no public health service for pets! All veterinarians work on a private basis and charge for their services, even if no treatment is given.

Many insurance companies offer pet health policies and these are an excellent "safety net" if money is short.

choosing a veterinarian

Choosing a veterinarian for your cat is as personal as selecting a doctor to treat and care for a person's health. Other cat owners in your area can probably make personal recommendations, a quick and easy way to find a veterinarian that suits you and provides excellent service. However, you may wish to consider what kind of services the practices offer and which appeals to you.

Smaller practices are often more personal—you will get to know the veterinarian and nurses and they will grow to know your cat. This personal touch is very important if your cat experiences minor health changes, as the veterinarian will be able to compare him or her from one visit to the next.

Larger practices may not offer such personal service, but are likely to have more facilities, such as laboratory analysis. Veterinary hospitals can perform operations on site, and have the facilities to give your cat post-operative care.

emergency service

No matter the size of the veterinary practice, it is imperative that they offer after-hours emergency service. Sometimes this is provided by several local veterinarians working together using a duty rotation system. In large

below *Early visits to the veterinary surgery can set your cat's view of them for life.*

practices, the partners themselves are often on a night rotation to treat emergency cases. Ask your practice about their policy—in an emergency all you will want to worry about is your cat.

care and consideration

Far more important than opening times, facilities, and decor is the care that the veterinarians and staff offer your pet. Your kitten's first experience of going to the veterinarian is likely to involve being given a first or second vaccination by injection. Most veterinarians are expert at this and can administer the vaccine quickly and without trauma.

However, it is far more pleasant for your kitten if the veterinarian takes a little time to get to know him and checks him over thoroughly before giving the injection. A pleasant "basketside manner" is not essential for good medical care but it makes a big difference to your kitten's view of the whole experience.

right *The surgery's staff are as important as its facilities.*

safe transport

Always transport your kitten to and from the veterinarian in a suitable carrying container or carrying basket. Kittens can become lost or possibly hurt if they jump from your arms.

protecting your kitten

below Your kitten's first encounters with a veterinarian will be for essential vaccinations.

why vaccinate?

As a responsible owner, you will want to ensure that your kitten remains as healthy as possible throughout his or her life. Vaccinations are available against four major infectious diseases: feline leukemia, cat flu, feline enteritis, and chlamydia.

Sadly, the numbers of cat owners who ensure that their pets are vaccinated against disease is generally far less than among dog owners, possibly because feline diseases have less historical significance and media coverage than canine distemper and parvovirus. However, the feline parvovirus (panleukopenia virus), the cause of feline enteritis, although rare thanks to owners who persist with vaccination programs, can still be fatal in unprotected kittens and young cats.

Cat flu—or more accurately, feline upper respiratory disease complex—has two main causal agents, feline calicivirus and feline herpes virus, and can cause such extreme debilitation that recovery is unlikely, particularly in young and old cats. A more recent addition to the cat vaccination program protects against feline leukemia virus. In addition to causing tumors and fatal anemias, FeLV infection results in suppression of the immune system and is frequently associated with other serious and life-threatening infections.

Unlike cat flu and enteritis, which can be picked up from the environment, feline leukemia seems to be spread only

Handling and restraint are often necessary in veterinary treatment—accustom your cat early.

by direct cat-to-cat contact. The risk of contracting FeLV infection in a boarding cattery should therefore be negligible and, consequently, such establishments insist only on vaccinations against feline enteritis and flu. As a significant number of cats are vaccinated only because their owners are going away on vacation rather than for their own sake, vaccination against leukemia is, as yet, much lower than it should be to fully protect the cat population against this fatal condition.

Chlamydia psittaci var. felis is a common cause of conjunctivitis (inflammation of the lining of the eyelids), resulting in a puffy swelling of the conjunctivae, eye discharge, and much discomfort. Infection can be passed from mother to kittens very early in life, and if not treated early enough it can cause permanent scarring and distortion of the eyelids, blockage of the tear ducts, and sometimes severe, possibly blinding,

damage to the eyeball itself. The chlamydia vaccination has recently been incorporated into a single injection to protect against all the major cat diseases.

Generally, a first vaccination should be administered at eight to nine weeks of age, followed by a booster dose at 12 weeks old. Since entering a new home and the first vaccination are the biggest challenges a young kitten will experience, allow your pet a few days to acclimatize with you before taking him for the first injection.

worming your kitten

Kittens should be routinely wormed against roundworm (*Toxocara cati, Toxascaris leonina*), parasites that may be passed from mother to kittens via the milk, as well as being picked up from feces. Once out and hunting, cats can be infected by eating worm hosts, such as rats, mice, and birds, that carry immature stages of the roundworm.

Unlike the dog roundworm, which migrates through the body of the puppy as part of its life cycle, there is no evidence for risk of human infection from the cat roundworm.

Tapeworm infection is less common in kittens than in adult cats. The two main species, *Dipylidium caninum* and *Taenia taeniaeformis*, carry out the intermediate stages of their life cycles in fleas and rodents respectively. Unless a kitten has a heavy flea burden or has been weaned onto a diet of freshly caught mice, they are unlikely to show the tell-tale signs of rice-like tapeworm segments passed out in the feces until they are rather older.

Worms tend to vary from country to country and can even be dependent upon local geography. Effective multi-worming preparations in the form of tablets, granules, or oral suspensions should be obtained from your veterinarian.

flea protection and neutering

There are over 2,000 species of flea worldwide! In warm regions and the favorable conditions of our homes, the life cycle of the flea can be completed in as little as 12 days. The adult flea must remain on the host animal to feed and mate and represents, at any one time, only 5 percent of the total flea population. The remaining 95 percent consists of eggs, three larval forms, and pupae that develop wherever the cat has access in the home. In an average lifetime of a few weeks, the female flea can lay over 2,000 eggs; if left untreated, a few fleas on a newly acquired kitten can rapidly explode into several thousand!

Skin irritation from flea bites is often worsened by the cat nibbling and licking the area, and extensive hair and skin damage can result. Cats can become allergic to the saliva of the flea, when scabby rashes (miliary eczema) erupt all over the body. As

below *Ruffling the fur of your kitten while he or she is on a white surface reveals any flea droppings.*

egg-producing female fleas need to ingest 15 times their bodyweight in blood every day, a heavy burden of fleas on a young kitten can cause significant blood loss and serious clinical anemia.

There are a variety of preparations on the market to control this very successful parasite. The most potent and effective of flea treatments are available only by prescription from your veterinarian. As dogs and cats share the same fleas, your chosen method of flea control must be applied to all cats and dogs in the household.

Insecticides come in the form of shampoos, powders, sprays, and liquid "spot-on" preparations. Powders are messy to apply and the patient's coat must be thoroughly brushed afterward; shampoos are not tolerated by the average kitten and cat; liquid "spot-on" preparations are applied in small quantities directly onto the kitten's skin and are the most effective.

The home should also be treated. Use a suitable long-acting insecticidal spray and thoroughly vacuum-clean to remove as many eggs and larvae as possible.

Particularly useful for multi-animal households are non-insecticidal methods of flea control that blocks the development of one of the larval stages of the flea, thus breaking the life cycle. This treatment can be given to cats in the form of a liquid suspension, given monthly with or after food, or, even more conveniently, by a single injection effective for six months. Once all adult fleas are dead, this method alone should prevent reinfestation of the home.

neutering

The advantages and timing of neutering your pet can be discussed during your kitten's first veterinary check-up. It is also advisable to ask your veterinarian to check the animal's gender to prevent any surprises later on, as it is not uncommon for mistakes to be made when tiny newborn kittens are examined by the breeder.

Unlike the bitch, entire (unneutered) queens come into season, or estrus, for up to five days every three weeks throughout the spring and summer months. A non-fertile period (anestrus) usually follows, during the short winter days. The first season occurs on average at eight to nine months of age, but for kittens maturing in February and March with increasing daylight hours, it can be considerably earlier. Eggs are released from the ovary only after the stimulation of mating, when the signs of estrus immediately subside; it is possible for a young cat to have been mated and become pregnant in springtime without the owner being aware that the first season had occurred!

Unless you are sure you can find suitable homes for a litter of kittens, female cats should be spayed by the age of five-and-a-half to six months.

right Many forms of medication, such as this non-aerosol spray, are available to control the flea population.

There is less urgency in arranging castration of the male. Testosterone-related territorial behaviors, such as spraying strong-smelling urine and fighting, do not usually manifest until after a year of age. Male cats do, however, become sexually mature before this age, so if you own both male and female kittens, it is advisable to neuter both at the same time.

dental care

Dental disease is a frequently overlooked cause of chronic discomfort in the older cat. Bad teeth and infected gums can also increase the severity of other age-related conditions. Certain breeds, particularly the Orientals, seem prone to very early gum disease and tooth decay.

Preparing yourselves and your kitten with daily handling of the head and mouth and making sure you can safely touch the teeth and gums will make later preventative measures much less stressful. In wild cats, the action of chewing all parts of the prey, including fur, skin, tendon, and bone, keeps the teeth free of plaque and tartar and the gums healthy. In the domestic cat, fed almost entirely on prepared cat food, this natural cleansing does not occur—even eating crunchy biscuits may not exercise teeth and gums in the same way.

Several brands of toothpaste are available for cats, some with an enzymatic action to kill bacteria in the mouth—rather than the abrasive action of our paste—and they are usually flavored to make them more palatable. They can be applied with specially designed soft toothbrushes or with a bristled finger-stall, which may be more acceptable to the cat, as it appears to be part of your hand. Although cleaning your pet's teeth twice per day is ideal, this may be difficult to fit into most people's lives. However, even a thorough brushing once per week does much to prevent plaque and tartar build-up, and later, disease.

what to feed

Cats are notoriously fussy eaters. Before you know what is happening, your new acquisition may have trained you into buying or cooking special foods, simply by refusing everything else. The less time you have on your hands, however, the less likely you are to succumb to

right *Cat toothpaste is flavored to make it more palatable.*

this ploy and it is certainly better for the cat's long-term health if you have the attitude "eat it or starve"!

Food fixations can lead to vitamin and mineral imbalances, and excess fat and protein intake. Although it seems contradictory, cats that become obese later in life usually start out as extremely picky eaters. This is because their owners' understandable concern that the animal is not eating enough can lead them to extraordinary and expensive lengths to ensure an empty plate.

Feeding one of the many well-balanced, complete foods is generally preferable to home-cooked meals. These are often available in different versions for various age ranges of cat and eliminate the need to give extra vitamin or mineral supplements. However, leaving these foods down all the time may lead to overeating—not only on the part of your pet but for neighborhood cats, too!

right *Rubbing the teeth and gums with a finger pad is one way to prevent decay.*

left *Pads, finger-stalls, and different types of brush can apply paste to your pet's teeth.*

administering medication

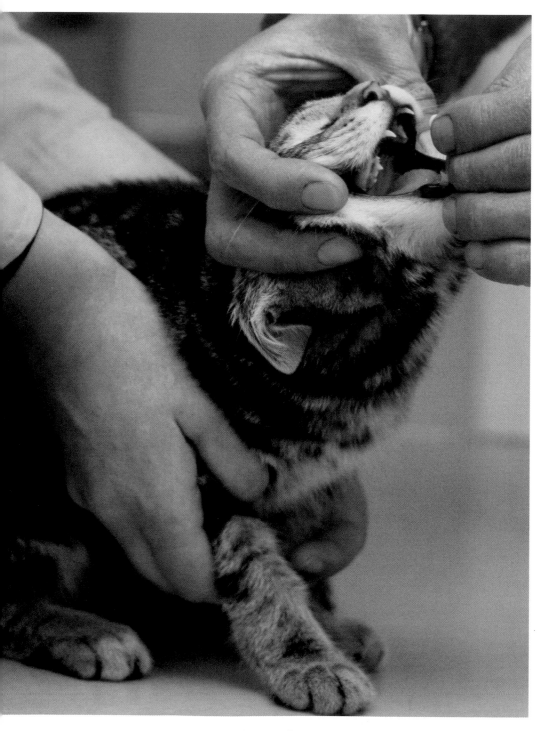

There can be few simple medical procedures that cause more trouble than giving a cat a pill! Some tablets are flavored to make them more palatable; of these, the yeast-like flavors seem to be the most acceptable. Liquid medication and crushed tablets can be disguised in tasty food, such as tuna fish or chicken, but a great number of cats will detect their presence and refuse the food. If this is the case or where there is a risk that the wrong animal will eat the treated food, it is necessary to administer drugs directly by mouth.

Frequent and thorough handling and examination from a very early age—grooming, opening the mouth to look at the teeth, and peering into the ears—generally renders a kitten more amenable to the application of medicines later in life. However, it still requires a certain knack and dexterity to give a tablet or apply ointment without causing stress to the cat and risking bites and scratches.

giving your cat a pill

1. Don't attempt to sneak up on your cat or kitten, in the vain hope that he or she will not know what you are doing. Instead, hold the cat securely on a hard surface of suitable height (a kitchen work-surface, for example). An assistant is recommended, to control

left *Firm, careful handling is required to make administering medication as stress-free as possible.*

the body and particularly the front legs of the cat, for any procedure involving the head. For fractious cats, wrap the body and legs firmly in a large towel for better control.

2. To give a tablet (if right-handed), hold the head firmly with the palm of the left hand resting on top of the head. Your left hand's thumb and forefinger should be midway along the upper jaw, the third and fourth fingers following the left side of the jawline to the angle of the jaw and side of the head, and the little finger lying across the back of the neck, toward the right side of the head. Grasping firmly, the head can be tilted vertically and the mouth will automatically open.

3. With the tablet held between the thumb and forefinger of the right hand, gently pull the lower jaw downward with the fourth finger while keeping the head held firmly vertical with the left hand. Drop the pill to the back of the mouth and push it directly down with the right forefinger, keeping the finger parallel with the teeth.

4. Close the mouth with the left hand and keep the head tilted upward until the cat is seen to swallow.

applying eye drops or ointment

1. Support and steady the cat's head with the fourth and little fingers of the left hand under the jaw and the third finger behind the head, while widening the lids with the thumb and forefinger.

2. Squeeze the required number of drops or a line of ointment onto the surface of the eye and gently massage the lids to disperse the application. Ointment is generally easier to apply if the tube is warmed in the hand for a few minutes first.

applying ear drops or ointment

When applying ear drops, it can be very difficult to prevent the vigorous reflex shaking of the head that any fluid entering the ear canal will induce. It is essential, however, to keep the cat's head still for a minute or so to allow the medication to penetrate to the horizontal part of the ear canal.

1. Hold the cat's head in the same way as for applying eye drops, but hold the tip of the relevant ear firmly between the thumb and forefinger while inserting the nozzle into the top of the ear canal and squeezing in the medication.

2. Maintain a firm hold on the tip of the ear until the base of the ear has been gently massaged to aid dispersal of the drops or ointment. Any wax or debris lifted into the upper parts of the canal by the fluid can be wiped away with a cotton ball.

common **health** problems

hereditary diseases

The naturally bred domestic short- or longhaired kitten (or "moggie") is unlikely to suffer any inherited or genetically based disease that might affect their fitness. Even in the artificially selected pure-bred kitten, such conditions are far less common than in their canine counterparts. One inherited condition seen on occasion is polydactyly—the presence of extra toes. Such kittens can look very appealing, with their apparently huge feet, but surgery may be required later if, for example, abnormal nail growth causes damage and pain.

Most cat breed standards deviate little from the "normal" cat shape and defects of conformation are relatively rare. Breeds such as the Persian, however, where human selection has resulted in exaggerated facial features, can suffer corneal ulcers and defective tear drainage, narrowed and distorted nasal passages, undershot jaws, and malaligned teeth. The likelihood of such supposedly desirable features causing problems in the future is frequently evident in the eight-week-old kitten and owners should be made aware of them at the first veterinary examination.

congenital problems

Congenital problems are present at birth but not necessarily inherited. Common problems detected in the young kitten include umbilical hernia, where the abdominal wall has failed to close completely. Varying amounts of abdominal contents can protrude through the wall, from a small bulb of abdominal fat to a whole loop of intestine protruding under the skin over the umbilicus. Surgery to correct such defects may be necessary and is usually done at the same time as neutering, unless there is an immediate risk to the kitten.

Male kittens may have only one testicle or, less commonly, no testes descended fully into the scrotum (cryptorchism). If the testes are retained in the abdominal cavity, such kittens may require surgery akin to spaying a female cat to locate and remove them.

parasitic infestation and infection

If preventive treatment has not been carried out by the breeder, early disease problems may include external and internal parasites, such as fleas, lice, and worms. Excessive shaking and scratching of the head and ears filled with black, crumbly wax are typical symptoms of ear mites (*otodectes*), which are transferred from the mother as soon as the kittens' ear canals open after birth.

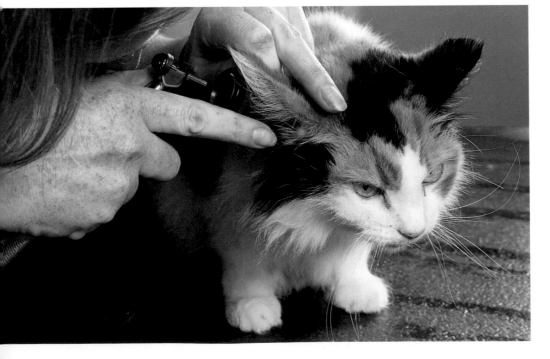

left *Ear mites can result in blood blisters or tumors if not detected and treated early.*

As cats and kittens often tolerate ear mites remarkably well, the infestation may go unnoticed until a more sensitive family dog begins to scratch his ears shortly after bringing a new kitten home. Intense scratching and subsequent damage to the ear flap (pinna) and the blood vessels within it may result in an aural hematoma, or blood blister. Even if surgically drained, such hematomas frequently leave the ear scarred and misshapen. In addition, long-term inflammation may predispose the kitten to the formation of ear polyps, or benign tumors of the ear canal, later in life.

Patches of thinning hair with non-itchy, flaky skin, often on the ears, face, and paws may indicate infection with ringworm. This is not a worm but a fungal infection, deriving its name from the typical ring of inflammation seen on human skin. Several weeks of treatment with a drug that prevents the fungal elements spreading into new cells, while infected skin cells are shed, is required. Ringworm is a zoonosis—an infection that can pass from animals to humans—and although it does not readily infect human skin, hands should always be thoroughly washed after handling infected cats and kittens.

Young kittens are frequently seen with watery or creamy discharge from one or both eyes, which may be accompanied by half-closed eyes and inflammation of the conjunctiva. If the kitten is otherwise bright and well, the cause is likely to be chlamydia; if the kitten is lethargic, less hungry than usual or not eating, sneezing, and running a temperature, it may have cat flu. Antibiotics, though not effective against the flu viruses themselves, help to keep any secondary infection at bay. Supportive treatment—force-feeding highly nutritious convalescent diets, for example—may be necessary to help the kitten's immune system fight the infection.

below *The circle on the head of this Tonkinese should be checked by a veterinarian for ringworm.*

stomach upsets and viruses

Stomach upsets in the form of diarrhea, with or without vomiting, are very common in kittens, particularly during their first few days in a new home. Even if their diet is kept the same as that given by the breeder, the stress of a new environment often results in intestinal disturbances.

Diarrhea can also occur as the production of the enzyme necessary to digest milk ceases as kittens grow older, or can be caused by the continuing presence of intestinal worms and other infections, such as the protozoan, *Giardia*, or toravirus, often associated with prominent third eyelids.

A small amount of fresh blood passed with the stool is not uncommon and seems to be of no significance so long as it occurs only infrequently, the stool is normal in consistency, and the cat appears well. At the first sign of any upset, the kitten should be starved of food for 24 hours. Light food, such as boiled chicken or fish, should be offered for two to three days, which is often sufficient time for the gut to settle down without further treatment. If, however, the diarrhea persists, is accompanied by vomiting, or the kitten is refusing food and fluids, prompt veterinary attention should be sought.

sore mouth
Kittens lose their baby (deciduous or milk) teeth at the age of four-and-a-half to five months and this may be accompanied by inflammation and mild infection of the gums (gingivitis). Most

left *Sore gums are a common side effect of the loss of milk teeth and growth of permanent ones.*

below *In its advanced stages, FIV causes fluid to accumulate in the chest, obvious when compared to a healthy cat. By this time it cannot be cured, but thankfully FIV is rare.*

kittens only suffer gingivitis during teething and the gums return to normal once the adult teeth have erupted.

However, in a small proportion of animals the inflammation persists into adulthood, resulting in intermittent oral pain, the need for frequent courses of antibiotics and anti-inflammatory drugs, and early tooth decay. Gingivitis that does not respond to treatment may be indicative of the feline immunodeficiency virus (FIV or "feline Aids"); your veterinary surgeon may suggest a blood test to eliminate this possibility.

viral infections

Poor growth, pallor and weakness may accompany infection with the feline leukemia virus (FeLV), as well as FIV, and the incidence of these infections varies in different areas. In the young kitten, such infections are likely to have been transmitted from the mother in the womb and, as the diseases they cause are nearly always fatal, euthanasia may be the kindest

option in a kitten who already shows symptoms. As both FeLV and FIV affect the immune system's ability to protect the body from infection, other conditions, such as feline infectious peritonitis (FIP) and feline infectious anemia (FIA), may be found in association with them.

toxoplasmosis

Toxaplasma gondii is a protozoan tissue parasite whose definitive host is the cat but which can affect humans. Although it generally causes mild symptoms of malaise and fever in both cats and humans, debilitated or immuno-suppressed individuals may develop a much more severe or even fatal illness.

Damage to the developing fetus may occur if a pregnant women is exposed to infection for the first time during the first three months of pregnancy. Contrary to popular belief, cats are not the primary source of infection to humans and pose little risk even if they are carriers of the parasite. The majority of human infection is picked

up from contaminated soil or drinking water or by eating infected, undercooked meat.

growths and tumors

Kittens and young cats are rarely affected by growths or tumors. An exception is lymphosarcoma, commonly associated with the FeLV virus. Lymphosarcoma can affect many different organs in the body but in cats under a year old is most likely to develop in the thymus gland in the front of the chest cavity. Thymic lymphosarcoma should be a suspected condition in any young cat with weight loss and breathing difficulties and is confirmed by radiography of the chest.

Naso-pharyngeal polyps—small fleshy growths originating from the eustachian tubes—are occasionally seen in kittens and, in their position above the soft palate, cause gagging and a snoring respiratory noise. They are surgically removable, resulting in a dramatic and complete resolution of symptoms.

injuries and urine **infection**

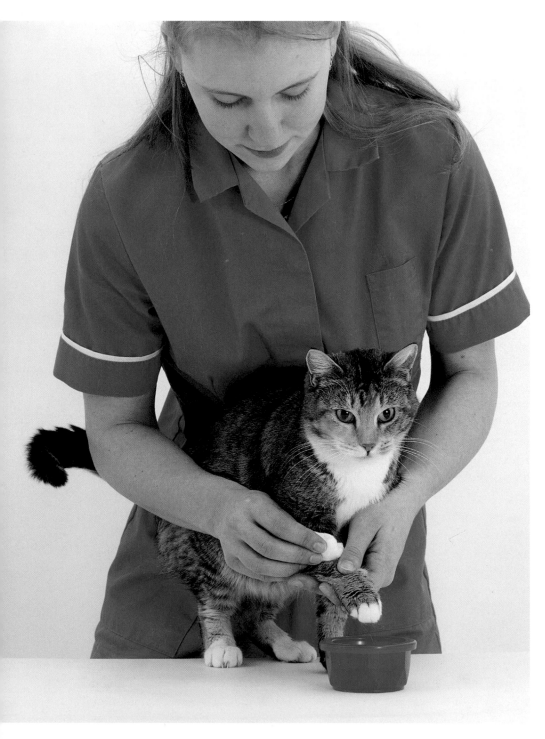

Once kittens start to venture outside the home, they are at risk from the single most common problem presented to veterinarians: the cat bite abscess. Infection carried on the canine teeth of cats is injected deep under the skin during a fight; whether an abscess develops depends on the resistance of the individual cat. Although almost all cats allowed outside get bitten at some time(s) in their lives, some are considerably more prone to developing abscesses.

If you know that your cat has been involved in a fight and a bite is likely, finding the wound, small though it may seem, bathing it in salt water, and taking the cat to your veterinarian for a precautionary antibiotic injection greatly reduces the risk of an abscess. If an abscess does develop, veterinary advice should always be sought. If it does not burst on its own, surgical lancing under general anesthesia may be necessary and antibiotics are nearly always required to ensure clean healing.

urinary tract infection
Cystitis, typified by increased frequency of and pain on passing urine, is a common condition in cats of all ages. Although it can be caused purely by bacterial infection, urine

left *Cleaning a wound and administering antibiotics usually prevents an abcess.*

samples frequently reveal abnormalities in the acidity and composition of the urine that result in crystal and bladder stone formation. Secondary infection is nearly always present, so treatment with antibiotics and special diets to correct the pH of the urine (preventing the precipitation of crystals) is required to prevent frequent recurrence of the condition. In male cats there is significant risk of life-threatening urinary obstruction if a crystal becomes lodged in the narrow urethra. Any male cat who seems unable to pass urine should therefore be treated as an emergency case.

Some cats react with cystitis-like symptoms to stressful situations and this should be suspected if the symptoms do not respond to antibiotics and no abnormalities are found in the urine.

unusual behavior in females

Veterinarians are frequently consulted regarding the young female cat who has suddenly begun to writhe around in an alarming fashion and cry out as if in extreme agony. Rather than heralding the onset of some non-specified disease, it nearly always transpires that these cats are simply in season—the dramatic and vocal signs are designed to attract tomcats from far and wide!

when to call the emergency veterinarian

If you suddenly become concerned about your kitten and are unsure whether the problem constitutes an emergency, it is always safer to immediately telephone your veterinarian for advice, whatever the time of day or night. It is far better for your fears to prove groundless than to delay treatment for a potentially serious illness or injury.

Be prepared to be asked to take the kitten directly to the veterinarian, should your veterinarian consider that immediate attention is necessary, even if this means arranging special transport or child care. Although it may seem initially more convenient to ask for a house call, the equipment and medication required to treat a possible emergency will only be available at the clinic. In addition, house visits add considerably to your bill.

road traffic accidents

Any cat or kitten suspected of being involved in a road traffic accident (RTA), even if any visible injury appears minor, should be checked by a veterinarian as soon as possible. It is possible for badly injured cats to run away after such an accident and for internal damage to pass unnoticed. Cats can also appear barely conscious following a road accident, yet recover remarkably quickly when given treatment to counteract shock.

Always telephone your veterinarian first to let them know that you are on your way, so that the necessary preparation for emergency treatment can

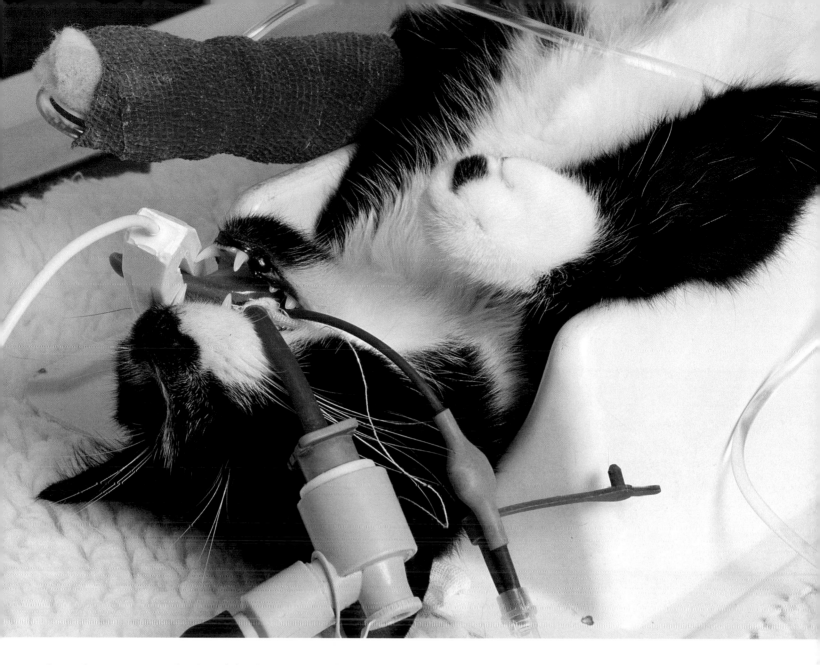

be made. A cat may need to be stabilized with the administration of intravenous fluids before further investigation, such as taking X-rays, can be carried out.

Common injuries following an RTA include a ruptured diaphragm, where the thin muscular sheet separating the chest and abdominal cavities becomes torn, allowing contents of the abdomen, such as liver and intestines, to enter and fill the chest cavity. Such cats typically show great difficulty in breathing, as the lungs are compressed by the presence of other organs. It is possible to surgically repair such damage but not without considerable anesthetic risk. However, once a cat has recovered consciousness after such

an operation, they normally show enormous resilience and usually begin to eat within 24 hours.

Bony structures are commonly damaged in road traffic accidents, ranging from fractures or dislocations of the spine, resulting in paralysis of the hind limbs and euthanasia on humane grounds, to broken toes, which usually heal on their own.

The pelvic area is frequently involved in trauma, either of the pelvic bones themselves, the hip joints, or the junction between the tail and the portion of spine to which the pelvis is attached (the sacro-caudal junction). Many pelvic injuries heal on their own, as long as the cat is given adequate opportunity to rest by confinement in a hospital cage. If the spinal cord is traumatized at the level of the pelvis, however, the nerve

supply to the bladder may be irreversibly damaged, resulting in paralysis of the bladder.

Growth of bones in all young animals is allowed by the presence of uncalcified, soft areas, or epiphyses, which are situated at each end of the bone. As these growth plates are weaker than hard, calcified bone, epipyhseal separation occurs frequently in kittens and young cats rather than fracture of bone. The most commonly affected epiphyses are at either end of the femur, or thigh bone. Surgery is generally necessary to repair such damage. Mid-shaft fractures may need a metal pin or plate to realign the bone and allow satisfactory healing.

falls, foreign bodies and wounds

If a cat falls, the righting reflex usually ensures that they land with all four feet on the ground. Usually, the legs are protected from damage, since shock is absorbed through the joints. However, the momentum of the fall can cause the cat's head to hit the ground nose-first and the force thus generated can be enough to damage the lower jaw or split the roof of the mouth (the hard palate). A telltale nose bleed following a fall should always prompt a thorough inspection of the cat's mouth.

foreign bodies

Paroxysms of coughing, gagging, and retching, often thought to indicate "something stuck in the throat," may be symptomatic of an upper respiratory infection. If, however, the cat seems unable to eat or drink, there may be some foreign material present in the pharynx at the back of the mouth.

Most commonly, examination under general anesthesia reveals a blade of grass lodged over the soft palate, which is likely to have been swallowed, regurgitated, and then become stuck. Grass seeds, notorious for penetrating dogs' feet, can become wedged behind the third eyelid of the cat, causing extreme discomfort and ulcerative damage to the surface of the cornea. If a cat is unable to open an eye that is

left *The self-righting reflex cannot always save a falling cat from harm.*

watering profusely, examination under local anesthetic is necessary to eliminate this possibility.

cuts, bites and stings

Tears in the skin can be caused by the cat catching itself on protruding nails or barbed wire. As the skin of a cat is very elastic and retracts after damage, the holes are often much larger than they first appear. Although there may be little bleeding, cleaning the wound and suturing under anesthetic is often required.

If you discover a wound or any injury that might require anesthesia, it is sensible to withhold food from the cat before veterinary examination so that such procedures are not delayed. Although cat fights usually result in only minor damage in the form of puncture wounds, occasionally the third eyelid fails in its protective function and deep scratches or punctures to the surface of the eye are made. Thorns may also penetrate and remain embedded in the cornea, needing surgical removal.

Sudden and sometimes quite alarmingly large swellings might be noticed on the face or paws of kittens and cats, often after they have been playing outside. These lumps are often not particularly painful and, when squeezed, leave an impression or dent. Such edematous swellings are nearly always caused by an insect sting, resulting in a release of histamine and typical anaphylactic response. Although rarely affecting the cat other than to cause minor discomfort, very occasionally systemic anaphylaxis and shock can result, particularly with successive stings, so a veterinary check-up and administration of antihistamines and anti-inflammatory drugs is generally recommended.

Too often, cats are brought into the vet suffering from injuries caused by air gun pellets. Sadly, a few individuals consider it amusing to

shoot at cats with air rifles and how seriously the police take such incidents varies enormously from area to area. It is more luck than good judgment that many air gun pellets cause relatively little damage and their presence is often discovered by chance when a cat is x-rayed for another purpose. Pellets can, however, lodge in vital structures such as the

above *Grass seeds can become stuck in the throat or even behind the third eyelid.*

eye and spinal cord or penetrate the gut, resulting in leakage of intestinal contents and cause life-threatening peritonitis. They can also shatter bone, making subsequent repair extremely difficult.

vomiting and poisoning

A cat of any age that has not eaten for more than three days should be seen promptly by a veterinarian. Whatever the initial cause of loss of appetite, cats are prone to liver damage if they remain inappetant for any length of time. It is therefore very important that nutrition is maintained, by force-feeding if

below *Coughing is a serious sign—it can indicate a chest infection or asthma*

necessary, while investigation and treatment is carried out.

Diarrhea, particularly if accompanied by vomiting, can result in rapid dehydration in a small kitten that often needs correction with intravenous or subcutaneous fluids. Persistent vomiting may be caused by a spasm of the muscles that control stomach-emptying, in which case cats remain well in themselves though may lose weight.

An extremely lethargic cat that is vomiting and rapidly losing weight but not passing anything may have an obstructed intestine, which if undiagnosed and untreated is fatal. An obstruction can be caused if the gut folds in on itself—a condition called intussusception—as a result of excess gut movement (peristalsis).

Cats are less likely than dogs to swallow objects such as stones or chewed-up toys, but may play with and swallow pieces of wool or cotton. A loop of such material can get caught under the tongue but the loose end

continues to pass through the gut, causing the gut to fold up along the thread. Emergency surgical intervention is essential if the affected animal is to survive.

poisoning

Accidental poisoning is not common in cats as they are generally fastidious eaters, unlike the scavenging dog. However, eating rats or mice that have been killed by anticoagulant poisons, such as warfarin, can result in secondary poisoning and serious internal hemorrhage. Warfarin poisoning may be suspected in animals such as farm cats, who have access to poisoned bait and show signs of lethargy, anemia, and prolonged blood-clotting time. The antidote to Warfarin is vitamin K, which restores the blood's ability to clot.

If slug pellets containing metaldehyde are eaten they cause vomiting, lack of coordination, and convulsions. There is no specific antidote and supportive therapy, including sedation to control fits and intravenous fluids, is necessary to give a chance of recovery.

respiratory problems

Any difficulty in breathing should be treated as a matter of urgency. As cats are not expected to exercise in the same way as dogs do and generally take life at a much more leisurely pace, respiratory conditions and lung disease can be very much more advanced before symptoms become apparent.

Feline asthma is associated with a chronic cough and bouts of often extreme respiratory distress. The administration of oxygen by mask or

above *Playing with wool is natural, but if swallowed can cause the gut to fold up.*

oxygen tent can be a life-saving measure until anti-inflammatory drugs take effect.

The accumulation of fluid or pus in the chest cavity often follows respiratory infection and tumors in the chest. As the lungs are prevented from inflating in the normal way, severe respiratory distress results. Great care must be taken in handling such cats, as any stress or increase in demand for oxygen is likely to cause collapse. Tapping the chest to withdraw fluid may relieve the symptoms but often only temporarily. Sadly, the long-term outlook for any cat with free thoracic fluid is usually very poor.

kitten becomes cat

No matter how cute, cuddly, and playful your kitten is now, it is inevitable that he or she will soon grow up! Indeed, as soon as kittens lose their baby teeth at the age of about five months, they can officially be classed as adolescent!

Most kittens soon settle into a routine that will stand them in good

stead for the rest of their lives. As long as they feel comfortable in their environment, are confident being handled and petted, and are secure around their owners, kittens and cats will cope with the challenges that life brings on a day to day basis.

growing up

Cats tend to become much more interested in marking and maintaining territory as they head into adulthood.

Both males and females, neutered and unneutered, mark territory outside by spraying urine, scratching tree trunks and other posts, and leaving feces as boundary markers. These scent signals leave messages for other cats in the area, and although they will not prevent another cat from crossing a boundary, they give information about how long ago the "owner" marked the area, and possibly even who that cat was!

At this stage of their development, some sensitive cats may become anxious about the possibility of other cats coming into their home or crossing their territory in the yard. Fights with neighboring cats often confirm this, and the stresses of defending core territory may start to show.

Indoor urination and even defecation can be a clue that your cat is suffering from the stresses of coping as an adult, and these problems are best addressed by a feline behavior specialist as soon as possible.

where to go for help

There is now a network of specialists available to help with behavioral problems in cats. Ask your veterinarian for a referral if you feel that your cat needs behavioral help. Very often just understanding the cause of a problem is enough to be able to solve it and a single session with a pet behavior counselor may resolve even long-standing problems forever.

time flies

Kittens grow into cats almost before our very eyes. One minute they are playing on the carpet with a toy, the next they are out hunting real prey—for all the world an adult, independent, and sometimes aloof creature. Perhaps the very attraction of cats is that they combine the qualities of a domestic pet and a fascinating wild animal.

The relationships that we form with our cats are very important. Cats allow us to reveal our nurturing and caring sides, as well as providing company and the chance to laugh with a creature that loves attention and affection. Time is short while your kitten is young—make sure you enjoy it!

index